A Flight Plan
For Teaching Anyone Anything and Making It Stick

by

Sharon L. Bowman, M.A.

Applause for

Sharon Bowman,
teacher of teachers,
and trainer of trainers

• • • • •

"Sharon Bowman is phenomenal! After her training session with our staff, they were all hooked. The feedback? – 'Please give us more of Sharon!'"
Barbara A. Boyce, Director
Human Resources Development Program
North Carolina Community College System

• • • • •

"No one knows more about training tips than Sharon – no one! And no one walks the talk better than she does – no one! We have revelled in her enthusiasm, learned from her generous presentations, and grown as instructors, trainers, and humans as a result of her work."
Diane D. Cheatwood
Faculty Development Specialist
Community College of Aurora, CO

• • • • •

"Sharon's presentation to the most difficult audience of all – CORPORATE TRAINERS – was fun, positive, and full of wonderful interactive strategies for involving all learners. Everyone walked away with new tools and techniques for enriching their training delivery while laughing, smiling, and having a GREAT time!"
Susan Henderson
Training Development and
Employment Manager
Harrah's Reno Hotel and Casino, NV

• • • • •

"Sharon affirms what we do as teachers, trainers, guides!"
Chris Francisco
Senior Resource Specialist
Central Illinois Adult Education Service Center

3

• • • • •

"I'm indebted to Sharon for her insightfulness and practical ideas ... She moved huge stones (paradigms) and freed me to think about teaching in terms other than those with which I was familiar."

Deborah Treiber, Teacher
South Tahoe High School, CA

• • • • •

"Participating in one of Sharon's training sessions is a wonderful gift you can give to yourself. As a professional trainer, I've learned more from Sharon's workshops than from all my previous learning experiences combined."

Chris Waymire
Director of Training
Tecumseh Area Partnership, Inc., IN

• • • • •

"An outstanding teacher who, with her expertise and enthusiasm, is able to keep the attention of any audience."

Kathi Jensen, Assistant Principal
South Tahoe Middle School, CA

• • • • •

"Sharon is a skilled trainer who brings great energy and joy to learning. Her book is a delightful reflection of her style – almost as much fun as learning with her in person."

Karen Hewett, Director
Faculty, Staff and Organizational Development
Community College of Aurora, CO

• • • • •

"What a great difference Sharon's class made in my life as a trainer!"

Kathi Goodwin
Methodology Consultant
USA Group, Fishers, IN

• • • • •

"Flawless preparation and spirited, energetic delivery style ... just like her book, Sharon has a knack for making a connection with each person, making it meaningful, and doing it consistently."

Tim Christian
Training Manager
AT&T, Minneapolis, MN

And applause for Sharon's first book
"Presenting with Pizzazz"

• • • • •

*"This perky little paperback by an **Accelerated Learning Workshop** graduate contains a host of easy-to-apply ideas for getting learners more actively involved in their own classroom-based learning ... in style and content, a gem of a book."*

Tom Meier, Editor
The Accelerated Learning Newsletter, WI

• • • • •

"Right on the money. Clear, packed with ideas, and a must for any trainer."

Eric Jensen, Owner
Jensen Learning Corporation, CA

• • • • •

*"The best book on presenting that I've ever read. It's one thing to know HOW to do something. It's quite another to TEACH someone else to do it. Sharon does BOTH in **Presenting with Pizzazz.**"*

Edwina Frazier, Consultant
Partners in Success
Personal and Professional Development, MI

• • • • •

*"**Presenting with Pizzazz** not only provides great tips on how to energize and improve training classes and workshops, but it uses adult learning theory every step of the way ... a wonderful tool for every trainer and speaker's toolkit!"*

Susan Van Vleck
Professional Skills Developer
and Training Manager
AT&T, Phoenix, AZ

• • • • •

*"I have never found a training book with so many creative, easy-to-apply and fun exercises like **Presenting with Pizzazz.** Always keep this power-packed book close by because you'll use it countless times."*

Edward Leigh, M.A.
Professional Speaker and Publisher
The Humor & Happiness Catalogue, OH

• • • • •

*"**Presenting with Pizzazz** is a must for anyone in the teaching and training profession. Each time I read this little text I get new insights ... the message is fundamental to teachers and trainers everywhere."*
William F. Monaghan, B.A., LL.B, E.Ed.
National Adult Literary Agency
Galway Bay, Ireland

• • • • •

*"After reading **Presenting with Pizzazz,** I couldn't wait to begin utilizing the great techniques Sharon provides in her book. Thanks Sharon, for such a wonderful book!"*
Adele J Foster, Business Coach,
Consultant and Trainer
The Starting Point, NJ

• • • • •

"Sharon's wonderful book has impacted my presentations dramatically. Her simple, clear, user-friendly, and practical exercises have helped me connect with audiences better than any other book I've ever read. Colleagues and I now organize, Bowmanize, and humanize all our presentations."
Dan Coughlin, President
The Coughlin Company, MO

• • • • •

"A great resource for helping technical trainers create an environment of active learning!"
Phyllis Clayton, EdS
President
Clayton Gibson Co., KS

• • • • •

"The best instructional methodology book I have ever read."
Barbara A. Boyce, Director
Human Resources Development Program
North Carolina Community College System

• • • • •

"Having one of Sharon's books in a trainer's library is like spice in a chef's kitchen! How refreshing to see a trainer share so generously with her readers!"
Denise Bissonnette
Author, Trainer
Milt Wright & Associates, CA

A Flight Plan
For Teaching Anyone Anything And Making It Stick

Sharon L. Bowman, M.A.

Printed in the United States of America.

Second printing June 2000

Cover design and text layout by:
Ad Graphics, Tulsa, Oklahoma • 800-368-6196

Library of Congress Catalog Card Number: 97-092963

ISBN: 0-9656851-2-8

I'm most grateful to the following organizations for their valuable contributions to this book:

The Center for Accelerated Learning
David Meier, Director

Creative Training Techniques, Inc.
Robert Pike, President

The Duvall Center
Joyce Duvall, President

Excel, Inc.
Bernice McCarthy, President

And immense gratitude goes to those nearest and dearest to me whose gifts of advice, editing, time, and encouragement sustained me and without which this book would never have gotten off the ground:

Ross Barnett
Frances Bowman
Sue Channel
Gene Critchfield
Cindee Davis
Joyce Duvall
Curt Hansen
Colleen Hosman
Joanna Slan
Jan Thurman

Finally, special thanks to many teachers and school administrators across the United States, especially those in **Lake Tahoe Unified School District CA, Truckee Meadows Community College NV, Community College of Aurora CO,** the **Human Resource Development Program** of the **North Carolina Community College System, Region 18 Education Service Center TX,** and **San Juan Unified School District CA.** Also many thanks to the **Workforce Development and Employment and Training Institutes and Programs** and their supervisors, staff, and training participants all over the country.

This book is dedicated to
MY MOM
who, with much misgiving,
allowed her baby chick
to fly.

Contents

• • • • •

Come to the edge,
he said.
They said,
We are afraid.
Come to the edge,
he said.
They came.
He pushed them ...
and they flew.

...Guillaume Apollinaire

Introduction

•••••

It's 5:00 AM. and you're standing in pre-dawn darkness beside a perky red and white four-seater Cessna 172. A cool breeze ruffles the meadow grasses around the mile-high and mile-long airstrip of South Lake Tahoe, California. You are alone. You've just completed the pre-flight check of the little airplane, read through the list with a flashlight to make sure you didn't miss anything, and now you pause. Bathed in the cool, pine-scented air, you realize that, for the next six hours, you'll be flying this Cessna alone. By yourself. Drawing on everything you've learned in ground school and flight school. Flying over three-hundred miles of land you've never seen, stopping at two other airports that you've never flown to before. And there is no one else to depend on but yourself. No one to talk to, to question, to ask for help. This is your third and final long-distance solo cross-country flight. Final because, after this flight, you'll be signing up for the FAA flight exam to become a private pilot. But that's the future. Now, before climbing into the Cessna, a thought crosses your mind: **You know with absolute certainty that your success in this adventure relies upon giving each moment of the flight your total attention and your personal best.** You can't predict what will happen moment-by-moment as you pilot the airplane, **but you're sure that if you stay relaxed, alert, focused, confident, and draw on everything you've learned about flying, the journey will be a successful one.** You take a deep breath, send a prayer skyward over the dark mountain peaks surrounding the Tahoe airport, and strap yourself into the left seat, pilot seat, of the Cessna. The adventure has begun!

Your total attention.
Your personal best.

And that, my friend, is what it's like when you stand before a new class of students or a new group of training participants. It doesn't matter if you've given the class or training a hundred times before. **You still pause, take a deep breath, and remind yourself that your success in the adventure – and theirs – depends upon giving it your total attention and doing your personal best.**

In flying, "total attention" means being attuned at all times to the airplane: its gauge read-outs, its engine noises, its movement through the air. **In teaching anyone anything, "total attention" means being attentive to your learner's needs, being flexible enough to change your methods of instruction to match those needs, and checking for understanding often.**

"Doing your personal best" while piloting a plane requires you to have the knowledge you need to do the task. It also means taking care of yourself and your body so that you're in a state of relaxed alertness, confident in your ability to fly and to handle unexpected occurrences. *("Cessna 172, unidentified plane at 7500 feet, 5 miles out, opposite direction, 12:00." Translation: another plane is mistakenly flying at your altitude straight for your nose!)*

"Doing your personal best" while instructing others means that you know how to give information to other people so they can understand and use it. That implies knowing how to plan and present your information as well as knowing your subject matter. Of course it also means having the confidence to handle those little ULEs, i.e. *"Unexpected Learning Experiences."* *("Excuse me for interrupting your class, but we couldn't find the overhead projector you wanted, your handout materials have been delayed, and half of your students went to the wrong building and will be arriving here shortly.")*

How To Give It So They Get It is your ground school workbook, so to speak, to help you bring your total attention and personal best to your classes and trainings. ***It explains in user-friendly language how you and others learn.*** It shows you how your preferred learning style impacts the ways you teach, train, and give information to others.

Perhaps more importantly, this book teaches you how to use the styles map, a powerfully effective tool that will help you create successful learning experiences for all your students and training participants. In effect, it's your "flight plan" that will guide you in your own unique journey towards a distant learning destination. When you use the map to organize your delivery of information, you increase the active participation and long-term learning of your students.

Simply put, using the styles map is a practical way of helping people learn better and remember more.

> ***Nothing works all the time,***
> ***but the map will work***
> ***most of the time***
> ***for most of your learners***
> ***with satisfying success for them***
> ***and for you.***

By the way, a ton of research has been written about the styles map and about the basic ways people take in information (learn) and give out information (teach, train, present, speak, and communicate). This book just makes the research easy to understand and use. If you are into the more esoteric side of research, then check out the books in the bibliography and feast to your heart's content.

You can also use the styles map when you're teaching someone something on a one-to-one basis: showing a colleague or co-worker a new procedure, explaining something to your significant other, teaching your child a new skill, conducting a meeting with a new client or customer, in other words, anytime you have to give others information they need.

> *Anytime you explain something*
> *to another human being,*
> *or teach that person something,*
> *or help him learn something,*
> *you're a teacher,*
> *and this book is for you.*

You'll note that I use the words "teacher" and "trainer" synonymously. The words "student," "learner," and "training participant" are also synonymous. Don't get hung up on the words. *For the purposes of this book, anyone who gives information to others is a teacher and anyone who receives information from others is a student.*

As you read, you'll be doing some quick exercises, answering a few questions, and playing with the information while you learn. I encourage you to highlight, doodle, scribble notes, and scrawl your own reactions and insights across its pages. *You'll be learning faster and remembering more when you do.*

Let's do that now. Grab a writing utensil (a what?) and scribble two things you'll be learning from this book:

1.

2.

Could you do it? If so, bravo! Did you need to look back through the introduction to find them? That's okay too. Check to see if the two items you wrote had anything to do with the following:

1. *How you and others learn.*
2. *How to use the styles map.*

Let's do one more. In the box below, draw a doodle (yes, I said doodle!) representing something you really want to learn from this book. Your doodle can be a drawing, a line, a squiggle, a shape, anything to illustrate why you're reading this right now.

Now add a written sentence to your doodle explaining what it means. When you've done that, find a person (or family pet!) and show him your handiwork. Sounds silly, yes? You've just defined for yourself why you're reading this book. By doing that, you'll actually read with a more focused mindset since you know specifically what it is you want to learn. Good going!

There's a saying among pilots of small single-engine land airplanes: *"If you have time to spare, then go by air!"* At first, using the information here will take some time – time to learn it, to become familiar with it, and to put it into practical use. Give yourself permission to take the time you need to absorb it all. And, as with flying, you never can predict all the variables in a learning experience. So sometimes you have to let go of everything you know and *"fly by the seat of your pants."*

You may discover as you read this book that you're already using many of the ideas in it. If that's the case, now you'll know the reasons why they work for your students, and you'll be able to fine-tune what you already do well. In fact, you'll be delighted with how much richer your lessons and trainings will feel to you and your learners.

So what's the bottom line? Simply this:

**People learn in different ways.
So you have to teach them
in different ways
in order to help them learn.**

I hope that you enjoy the energy as well as the information in this book. And I hope that you'll share what you learn with your family, friends, and colleagues. ***Above all, I hope you'll get to experience the satisfaction that comes from knowing how to teach anyone anything and making it stick.***

One doesn't discover new lands
without consenting to
lose sight of the shore
for a very long time.

...Andre Gide

Your total attention;
your personal best.

...Sharon Bowman

Take what you can use
and let the rest go by.

...Ken Kesey

As soon as I can find a good position,
I intend to take a firm stand.

...Ashleigh Brilliant

Chapter One:
Sometimes You Don't Need
To Follow The Roads.

Chapter One:
Sometimes You Don't Need
To Follow The Roads.

· · · · ·

D o you know what this is?

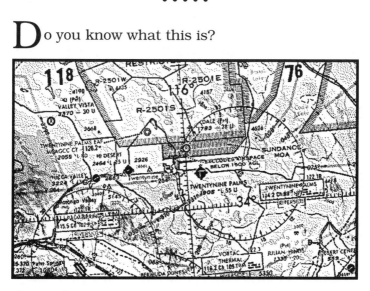

If you think it's a map, you're absolutely right. If you know it's a sectional, or aeronautical chart, you're a pilot or you hang out with pilots. Yes, it's the type of map that a pilot uses to plot her course when she creates a flight plan.

Eight years ago I used a map like this to chart the route of my first cross-country solo flight, from the South Lake Tahoe Airport in California to Walker Lake, Nevada, a distance of some one-hundred and seventy-five miles round trip over three valleys and two mountain ranges. I painstakingly drew the lines on the map and filled in the flight plan, then proudly took both to my flight instructor for approval.

Gary was a jovial sort of person, always kidding even when I'd make a major mistake – like bouncing the Cessna's nose-wheel *("Okay, Sharon, now that you showed the world how NOT to land, let's show everyone in the control tower what an A+ landing CAN look like!").* When he eyed the course I had plotted on the aeronautical chart, his eyes crinkled in amusement, he cleared his throat, looked kindly at me and said, *"Sharon, you're not quite clear about the concept yet. You're going to be flying an airplane. Airplanes don't need to follow the roads."* On the map, I had zig-zagged my way across Nevada following all the major state highways so that I wouldn't get lost, and in doing so added an extra hour and a half to the flying time.

Sometimes you don't need to follow the roads.

Think about that as a metaphor for teaching and learning. Following roads that have aged with time may not be the best and fastest way to reach your destination. The older the road, the more cracks, potholes, and broken pieces of asphalt. The older the road, the harder it is to travel it, and the longer it takes to get to where you want to go. And following roads when you're in an airplane is a complete waste of time.

Old roads represent outdated ways of teaching and learning that don't really work anymore, or that never worked well in the first place. The airplane stands for newer ways to give and get information that are fast, effective, and lasting.

What are these old roads I'm talking about? Here are seven of them. Seven worn-out roads. Seven traditional beliefs about teaching and learning that actually do more harm than good. Seven myths about learning that need to be discarded to make way for new and more successful ways to learn.

Seven Myths About Learning

MYTH #1: *Some portion of your anatomy must be in contact with a chair at all times in order to learn!*

FACT: *Your ability to learn diminishes in direct proportion to the amount of time you spend sitting.*

MYTH #2: *The person doing the most listening is doing the most learning.*

FACT: *The person doing the most talking – or moving or writing – is doing the most learning.*

MYTH #3: *Being a "sage-on-the-stage" – giving information in lecture format – is the best way to present information so that others learn it.*

FACT: *You remember only 10%-20% of what you hear. If you want someone to hear it, you lecture; if you want someone to really learn it, you become the "guide-on-the-side" and create different ways of presenting the learning.*

MYTH #4: *When you listen harder you remember more.*

FACT: *You learn and remember 80% - 90% of what you say and do. Therefore, in order to really learn anything well, you need to talk about it with others and do something with the learning a number of times yourself.*

MYTH #5: *The more serious the learning is the more you'll remember.*

FACT: *You'll learn best – and remember more – when you're having fun while learning. Fun is a necessary part of the learning process.*

MYTH #6: *A quiet room means people are learning.*

FACT: *Since you need to talk and move in order to learn, prolonged silence may indicate a state of "benign hypnosis" – when your eyes glaze over and your mind is a million miles away.*

MYTH #7: *Only the experts get to talk.*

FACT: *You come to a learning experience knowing a wealth of information you can share with others to help speed up the learning process for everyone.*

So what do you do when the old roads are beyond repair? When they're no longer fit to travel? It's obvious. You don't use them anymore. You find, or construct, new ones that will get you where you want to go, faster and more comfortably. **You learn new ways to give information to others, ways that will work easily, quickly, and with better long-term results.**

> **They always say**
> **that time changes things,**
> **but you actually have**
> **to change them yourself.**
> *...Andy Warhol*

> **If you want to win anything**
> **– a race, your self, your life –**
> **you have to go a little berserk.**
> *...George Sheehan*

> **The more sure you are,**
> **the more wrong you can be.**
> *...Ashleigh Brilliant*

Ground School

• • • • •

One of the greatest books around is the annual **FAA Flight Examination Questionnaire Workbook.** Why? Because it contains 500 questions from which fifty are randomly chosen as your FAA ground school flight exam. In other words, you have in your hands all the questions and answers to the written test! And the ground school instructor makes sure that he covers those questions *by teaching to the test.* So, if you answer all the questions in the workbook, and study from it, you can't fail – *success is virtually guaranteed!*

This is your chance to take a little test on what you've learned so far. And, just like the FAA workbook, *your success is guaranteed!* **More importantly, you'll move the learning into long-term memory by taking your turn at figuring out what you know and what you can do with it.**

1. The title of Chapter One refers to (circle an answer):

A. *planning a trip by air.*

B. *avoiding old roads when traveling.*

C. *old ways of teaching and learning that may no longer work for you and your students.*

Now check your answer:

For A and B: Oops!

For C: Right you are! Now for a harder one:

2. Label the following M for "Myth" or F for "Fact."

A. *The person doing the most listening is doing the most learning.*

B. *You learn and remember 80%-90% of what you say and do.*

C. *You remember everything you hear.*

D. *If the room is quiet and the learners serious, it means that learning is taking place.*

E. *Sharing information with others speeds up the learning process.*

F. *It's best to listen only to the experts because they're the ones with all the information.*

G. *Creating different ways of presenting information will help your learners "get it."*

H. *Go ahead and have fun – you'll learn more.*

I. *Gotta keep your bottom in a seat if you want to learn!*

Here are the answers: M F M M F M F F M. How did you do? If you got 100%, fantastic! If you didn't, correct any mistakes and change your score (that's insuring your success).

3. As a teacher, one practical way to use the information in this chapter is (highlight an answer):

A. *making sure your students know all the myths and facts about learning.*

B. *designing a learning experience so that your students spend some of their time out of their seats, moving and talking to each other about what they've learned.*

C. *deciding which road to take when going to work.*

Check it out:

For A: It might interest your students to know some of the myths and facts about learning, but it may not be that practical.

For B: Yes – you got it!

For C: Ahem!

4. From your reading of this chapter, what is one small change you're willing to make in what you do when you give information to others?

5. Call a friend or colleague on the phone and share your idea from question #4 with him. Then put the idea to use in your next class or training. Write the results here.

Chapter Two:
Get A New Map.

Chapter Two:
Get A New Map.

· · · · ·

Remember the aeronautical chart? Well, it has a warning printed on it in bold letters. It cautions: *"This map will become obsolete in one year. Do not use after May 1997. Get a new map."*

When you were a kid, you were given an armful of maps from your parents, schools, and cultures. Maps like how to be successful, what kind of person to marry, how to talk and behave, how to solve problems, what to eat, how to look, what's good for you, what's bad for you, and on and on. As an adult, how many times have you checked to see if your old maps still serve you? How many times have you scrapped an old map? How many times have you said to yourself, *"I learned that when I was a kid but it no longer applies to my adult life"*? **How many times have you acknowledged that the old map maybe never really worked that well to begin with – it was just the best thing around at the time?**

When it comes to teaching, old maps abound:

- *"I've always done it that way."*
- *"If it worked for me, it'll work for them."*
- *"When I was a kid ..."*
- *"That's the way it is when you go to school."*
- *"You have to make them learn."*
- *"This is just the way things are."*
- *"Learning is serious stuff. If they want fun and games, they can go to an amusement park."*

Guess what? It's time to scrap the old maps and:

Get a new map!

Why? Because the old maps were never designed around the way the human brain really learns; they were just the only ones available at the time.

Settle back. I'm going to tell you a story: Once upon a time, about 150 years ago to be somewhat exact, there lived a kindly gentleman named Horace Mann who had a fancy title – the Commissioner of Education for the state of Massachusetts – and who harbored a dream: *to educate all citizens in the United States of America.* Education, according to Mann, was the number one way to rid the country of its social ills: with a literate society there would be no unemployment (Mann assumed that citizens who knew how to read and write could always find jobs) and no crime (with all citizens working and making good wages, there would be no need for people to steal or otherwise lead lives of crime). Mann's intentions were honorable and his vision of an educated society, where a government-sponsored school system was accessible to all, was admirable.

There were a number of obstacles in the way of Mann's great dream. *One problem was the fact that he had to make his ideas financially palatable to the large agrarian communities.* Parents were skeptical about pulling kids away from the farms to get some "book learning." To do this, Mann had to set up a system that would educate the greatest amount of children for the fewest dollars. *He fashioned what he thought was the most brilliant solution to the problem: the class and grade system* which was patterned after a form of schooling in Europe at the time.

It made sense to Mann. With children of one age occupying one room, you could put as many children into that room as it could hold, and you could teach them all the same subject matter at the same rate. Furthermore, because they were all the same age, the learning would be uniformly the same. And the financial impact on the country would be minimal.

Again for financial reasons, Mann looked for a segment of American society who would work for the low teacher's pay he was offering and who would obey the males supervising the schools. He found single and widowed women willing to do both because they desperately needed the jobs. *So the stereotypical "school marm" was born and Americans now had a government-sponsored, low-cost educational system.*

As the class and grade system took hold, expenses for books and education materials were also kept at a minimum. Theoretically, with all children of one age in the same room learning the same thing at the same time, only one book was needed. *The teacher had "the book" and the children listened to her read or lecture from the book.*

An even larger obstacle to Mann's dream than the problem of finances – and one which today is still the undoing of the class and grade system – was the fact that *human beings, unlike factory parts and products, are not cut out of the same mold.* Put thirty kids of the same age in the same room and you have thirty different people learning things in different ways at different times with different levels of ability. *In other words, we are a mixed and motley sort of species that historically never did conform well to regimented factory-type systems of learning where everyone does the same thing at the same time.*

> *Imagine a widget factory where,*
> *when the widgets are on the assembly line,*
> *some of the them decide to hop off,*
> *to check out, to run away,*
> *to go home.*
> *Or some of them stay*
> *but refuse to move.*
> *Or some of the widget parts*
> *come to the factory damaged*
> *and it's your job to fix them*
> *and make them work again*
> *with some spit and glue*
> *and a few old tools.*
> *Imagine a widget that*
> *once it was sold,*
> *refused to get on the truck!*

In spite of this, the class and grade "map" had been marketed to the American society as "the way to learn." Leslie Hart, in **Human Brain and Human Learning,** summed up the prevailing thought at the time: *"Schools would teach and the children would learn. How could there be problems?"* And the predicted failure rate of this system? *"Below one-half percent ... (perhaps) not a single case of failure."* Hmm. Hindsight makes a wonderful teacher.

Simply put, the main components of this map were: you sit in a room with your peers, listen to a lecture, take notes, perhaps do some reading if there are enough books, and be quiet the whole time. Listening as the dominant form of learning was "in". Lecture as the dominant form of teaching was "in". Anything outside of the norm was suspect. Play as learning? Not on your life! Fun, laughter, talking to each other, moving around, enjoying the process? Forget it!

Even today, enjoyment is often considered a sign of frivolity, not learning. "No pain, no gain" is still a widely-accepted teaching/training motto. After a job skills training I facilitated, a supervisor was concerned that the training participants "had too much fun" and didn't learn anything because the training wasn't "serious" enough. Later she was pleasantly surprised to find out the number of new skills her staff members were putting into practice as a result of the training. In many circles, pleasure is still not considered a valuable and necessary part of learning.

Back to Horace Mann: the most insurmountable obstacle to his dream, and one which he had no idea even existed because there was little to no available research at the time to support it, was the fact that *the human brain learns and grows through continual external and internal changes, i.e. through diversity.* Hart describes the brain's optimum learning environment in one word: variety. A variety of people, learning levels, teaching methods, activities, interaction, learning strategies, content areas, resources, technology, you name it. The more varied, the merrier – and the better the learning.

Mann had no idea how the brain worked. It's as if he created a car factory but didn't know the first thing about a car engine. Poor Horace! *He marketed a method of teaching and learning that actually did the opposite: stifled and stunted the human brain's natural capacity and desire to learn.*

Well, so much for the 1850s. As teachers and trainers, where are we now? Still using a learning map that, if the truth be told, never worked that well in the first place. Still unfolding the crinkled and torn pages, looking for the old roads and guideposts to follow. Still patching it with tape and bandaids and hoping all the time it'll work better than it has. Still ignoring all the newest brain research around us that warns: **"This teaching and learning map is obsolete. Get a new map!"**

Thirty people once lived together
in a room in a big building.
They didn't sleep there,
but they came early every morning,
and they stayed all day,
except for two days
when they didn't come at all.
They sat in chairs,
and looked in books,
and wrote on papers.
They were trying to find out
about what was going on
outside their building.
Things happened out there
much faster than anyone
could report in books,
and much faster than anyone
could read in books.
So the thirty people had to spend
so much time reading
to find out what was going on
outside their building
that they had no time for looking outside,
or even looking around inside
at each other.
The people in the room
were always behind.
They never caught up.
They never got to know
each other very well.
They didn't even finish
any of the books.
...Anonymous

***You aren't stupid; they aren't stupid;
it's the process that's stupid.***

...David Meier

***School is bad enough,
but at least I'm not letting them
teach me anything.***

...Ashleigh Brilliant

Ground School

• • • • •

1. The title of chapter two is really about (check one):

A. *how to read a map.*

B. *getting rid of outdated maps.*

C. *hanging on to those dear old maps given to you by dear old dad (or mom, or school, or culture).*

D. *letting go of old ways of teaching and learning which never really worked that well to begin with – they were just the best ones available at the time.*

Check your own:

For A, B, C: Kidding around, aren't you?

For D: Absolutely!

2. Two obstacles to Horace Man's dream were (circle two answers):

A. *he had to set up a system that would educate the greatest number of children for the least amount of money.*

B. *he had to find enough materials so that each child had his own books.*

C. *he had no idea how the human brain learned and so designed a system that was contrary to natural learning.*

D. *he wasn't sure how the class and grade system would work.*

And the answers:

For A: Yes. The agrarian communities of the day were skeptical of "book learning" and couldn't afford to have their children removed from the farms to go to school year round.

For B: Nope. Materials cost too much so the teacher usually had "the book" and lectured, and the children listened and took notes.

For C: Right. This was his biggest obstacle, and the one that we still struggle with today.

For D: To the contrary, he thought the class and grade system virtually fail-safe.

3. **The most important thing you learned from this chapter was:**

4. **How do you think this information will affect what you do?**

5. **Share the story of Horace Mann with a friend or family member. What was her reaction to it?**

Chapter Three:
Where Do You Park
Your Car?

Chapter Three:
Where Do You Park
Your Car?

•••••

D o you drive your own car to work every morning? And do you usually drive the same route on the way to work? And when you arrive at work, if a certain parking place you like is available, do you find yourself parking in that spot everyday? And if, by chance, someone else gets to "your spot" before you, do you experience a twinge of, shall we say, irritation? *"How DARE he park in MY parking place? Why can't he find his OWN spot? Doesn't he know that's where I park? Now I'll be late for work because I have to look for another place."*

Most of us would prefer to park in the same spot than change parking places everyday. Sameness is easy; routines save us time. Changing things often, even something as simple as a daily habit like parking your car, can sometimes be difficult or at least irritating and time-consuming.

The same thing applies to the ways you take in information (learning) and give out information (teaching, training, communicating). Over time you find places inside your own head where you enjoy "parking your car," – ways of giving information to others that have become comfortable for you. You go to your favorite spot first because it's easier that way, and it saves you a lot of time and trouble. Often it's only when your "parking place" is taken – i.e., your comfortable ways of teaching no longer work as well – that you'll begin to explore other methods of teaching.

So where DO you park your car? Let's take a look at where you might go inside *YOUR* head in a new learning situation.

It's your birthday! You're really excited because the UPS truck has just delivered to your doorstep a large cardboard carton containing a special birthday present from your best friend. You drag the carton (it's very big and awkward to move) into your living room and cut away the cardboard with a knife. You step back and stare at about thirty black pieces of steel of various shapes and sizes. You realize that, after you assemble the pieces, you'll be the proud owner of a new exercise machine – one you've been wanting for months. You're thrilled because you're going to have the body of your dreams once you begin working out everyday. You can hardly wait to assemble the gift and get started on your dream body.

As you read the following four choices, choose the number that best describes what you would think and do next. You might even want to highlight the entire paragraph or paragraphs that most closely resemble you. By the way, there are no right or wrong answers here, only differences to explore. One way of learning isn't any better than another. Each way of approaching the situation has its own unique strengths.

1. At first you feel a little overwhelmed. The thought crosses your mind, "How in the world am I going to do this?" You suddenly realize that waiting awhile would make you feel better. Since you know you'll need time to figure it all out, you decide to put off doing it until the "right" moment comes along. And then you'll enlist the help of your significant other or friend so that it becomes a collaborative project. In any event, your first inclination is to wait and then talk to someone about putting the machine together. **Your motto is: "Learning together is better than learning alone."**

2. *You are pretty sure you can put it together once you have all the facts and details at your fingertips and a plan in your head. So the first thing you do is sit down with the instruction manual in your hands and read through it. You might even reread certain sections to make sure that you understand the procedure. Then you begin to sort out the pieces, organizing them neatly on the floor, and referring to the instruction manual as you go. You patiently proceed step-by-step constructing the machine with the manual as your infallible guide.* **Your motto is: "With enough knowledge you can accomplish anything."**

3. *You've put together so many things over the years that you feel something like an exercise machine should be pretty simple. Relying on your past experiences and common sense, you begin to move the pieces around, fitting them together as you go. You may refer to the instruction manual on occasion for a bit of clarification, but you're pretty comfortable doing it yourself without much input from the manual or from other family members. Common sense is your guide.* **Your motto is: "If it works, do it."**

4. *At first you groan, "Oh, no! It didn't come assembled! I hate having to do something step-by-step." So you dash outside and call across the fence to your neighbor, "Hey, friend, do you know how to put one of these together?" If your neighbor says "yes," you delegate the job to him. If he says "no," you resort to Plan B: you use the picture on the box as a guide and you begin to construct the machine from the hodgepodge of steel pieces littering the floor. You may even look at the pictures in the instruction manual as well (if you can find the instruction manual in the heaps of cardboard and steel). When you have the whole thing put together, and you notice two or three steel pieces still lying alone on the floor, you shrug and think, "Oh well, close enough. It'll do – I can use it anyway."* **Your motto is: "Try it and see what happens."**

Okay, okay, so you wouldn't choose any number! You wouldn't waste your birthday doing anything that smacked of drudgery. Besides, a lot would depend upon your birthday plans, your mood, or a host of other variables. So I'm reminding you here: *this is a metaphor for how you learn.* With that in mind, did you choose one number only? Or were you divided between two numbers? If so, which numbers were both like you? Could you see a number you definitely were *NOT?*

Speaking of metaphors, let's bring the metaphor of *"Where do you park your car?"* closer to home. **Why are you reading this book?** Highlight the paragraph below that best describes you.

1. You think it might help you become a better teacher so that you can more easily meet the learning needs of those around you. You hope to better understand where your students are coming from in terms of learning and how you can best help them. **You want your students to feel successful and happy while learning.**

2. You want more information about how people learn and you hope this book will give you the facts, backed up with the research and what the experts think (and who is this Sharon Bowman anyway? Does she really know her stuff?). **You want to have the right information to give to your students so that they will know what they need to know.**

3. You hope it will give you some useful and practical ideas you can use immediately in your work. Since you don't want to waste your time with details, you're probably skimming this book right now, keeping the little gems you can use and mentally tossing the rest. **You want to give those who learn from you real-life practical skills they can use.**

4. You want something to add to the energy and passion you have for what you do. Besides that, the book cover looks entertaining, the format interesting, and the cartoons fun. Anyway, you're always open to new ideas and have total confidence that you can take any idea and change it to make it your own. **You want to create new, exciting, and challenging ways of learning for yourself and your students.**

5. Your friend gave you the book and told you to read it. Or you know the author and feel obligated to read it.

6. You want to get a gift for a fellow teacher or trainer and this looked like a good one.

What was your preferred number and was it the same or different from the birthday metaphor? Maybe you chose two numbers to describe you. Or perhaps you feel that all four numbers are like you. Is there one number that definitely *ISN'T* you? (By the way, if you chose #5 or #6 because you say you aren't a teacher or trainer, remember that any time you give information to others, you *ARE* a teacher. Now go back and choose a different number.)

You're probably thinking, *"Hold on. It all depends on what I'm doing at the time as to where I go inside my head."* Congratulations! You get the prize! You're absolutely right. **The task at hand is the single most important variable in determining where you park your car.** Even so, over time you'll still notice a pattern (or patterns) in the ways you give and receive information.

Let's do one more. If it were up to you and you could choose one optimum way of learning that would best meet your needs when you take in information, which would you choose?

1. You learn best by checking out how you feel and how others feel about the subject – talking with one other person or a small group of people about the information and getting their ideas and input. Then you want time to take it all in. You learn by sensing and feeling who the teacher is as well as what the teacher says. Your favorite question is: "Why is this important to me?"

2. You learn best by reading, listening, and absorbing information *from experts in the field. Then you too want to spend some time by yourself sorting it all out inside your mind. You learn by analyzing information as you take it in. Your favorite question is: "What is it I really need to know?"*

3. You learn best by doing something immediately with the information *to see if you can use it in ways that work for you. You move quickly from thinking to action. You learn by acquiring skills that are practical and useful to you. Your favorite question is: "How can I use this?"*

4. You learn best by seeking out high energy experiences with other groups of people *who challenge you to think "out of the box." You combine new information with old to create new skills for yourself. You trust your intuition to guide you as you explore new ways of doing things. You learn by taking in information on many different levels. Your favorite question is: "What if I change it?"*

What was the number you chose now? Was it the same or different from the other situations? Do you see a pattern emerging? If your life depended upon telling someone, in two sentences or less, how you learn best, what would you say?

Are you beginning to get a clearer picture of how you learn? Want to explore this idea of styles a bit more?

You're in luck! It's time to give you the Bowmanized version of learning styles: You were born with a predisposition towards interacting with your world in a certain way (or ways). From infancy you began to explore the things around you in ways that helped you learn best. For example, as a baby you may have tentatively reached out to touch an object that interested you only after staring at it for some time. Or you may immediately have grabbed the object and stuffed it into your mouth. Or perhaps you picked up the object only after looking at mom or dad to make sure it was a safe thing to do. As a young child you may have needed to take your time and check everything out before moving or acting. Or you just may have jumped in with both feet and learned on-the-go.

Now combine this natural inclination towards responding in certain ways to the people and things around you (which is what learning is all about) with the maps you got from your family, friends, schools, and culture – maps that taught you about yourself and others, what was okay and not okay to do, what was okay and not okay to think, what was smart and what was dumb, what were acceptable and unacceptable ways to learn. The combination of your natural ways of learning and what others taught you about learning forms the basis of your preferred learning style or styles.

A mountain of research has been written about learning styles. There are as many styles-based teaching and training programs as there are labels for the different styles: personality types, management styles, behavioral preferences, leadership, communication, conversation and conflict resolution styles, and so on. Bernice McCarthy in **About Learning** gives the four styles numbers instead of word labels because they are easier to remember that way. Which is a blessing if you've ever delved into the Myers-Briggs or Kiersey-Bates material – great stuff but those darn initials are so hard to remember! And what do you actually *DO* with all that information anyway?

If hard-core research really excites you (and that will tell you something about *YOUR* preferred learning style!) check out the bibliography at the back of this book. If you're into the more streamlined version, and the practical uses of the research, read on.

Basically the research indicates that you learn in four major ways and the blend of those four styles is uniquely yours. Over time, you'll begin to notice patterns that point to one or more of the learning styles as your learning preferences or strengths. The other styles will be back-up places, or "stretching places" for you. *Stated again, you learn in all four ways; you just mix them up depending upon who you are, the task at hand, your age, gender, what has been okay and not okay to do in your own life, in other words, where you like to park your car.* As an adult, you can begin to see the patterns of learning you've embraced and which have become a large part of who you are.

Your preferred learning style or styles will in turn profoundly affect your teaching and training style. Furthermore, styles also impact how you communicate, solve problems, parent children, handle stress, play, work, plan, rest, grow, create – in other words, any human endeavor. A learning style preference is like the air you breathe – always there bathing you in its mixtures of smells, textures, sounds, and pressure. When talking about communication, Deborah Tannen in **That's Not What I Meant** points out, *"Conversation style isn't something extra, added on like frosting on a cake. It's the very stuff of which the communication cake is made."* **Similarly, learning styles are the foun-**

dation pieces used to design any effective learning experience. To ignore them is to leave 50% or more of your students struggling to learn (where do you think the old bell curve came from, anyway?).

So an understanding of styles is crucial to what you do. With that understanding comes Bernice McCarthy's observation: *"There is no one way to learn, and no one way to teach."* There is no such thing as "the right way." Instead, there are many ways and each way "honors" a certain part of yourself and your learners.

> **Well, stranger,**
> **there isn't any way**
> **you can understand me,**
> **but if you stop trying to change me**
> **to look like you,**
> **you might come to appreciate me.**
> **I'll settle for that.**
> **How about you?**
> ...*Kiersey and Bates*

> **A trifling matter,**
> **and fussy of me,**
> **but we all have our own**
> **little ways.**
> ...*Winnie the Pooh*

> **I may not be totally perfect**
> **but parts of me are excellent.**
> ...*Ashleigh Brilliant*

Ground School

• • • • •

1. Here are a few more characteristics of each learning style. As you read, highlight the sentences that describe you. Remember, you're a blend of all four styles but you'll probably find yourself highlighting more sentences in one or two of the lists. These style preferences also apply to your students as well. In any class or training, all four style groups will be represented by your learners. You'll see the following style characteristics in them also.

Learning Style One: Peacemaker

You prefer working with people rather than data and things.

You listen to others before making your own points.

You need to connect personally with other people involved in the learning experience.

You like personal attention and feedback.

You process information through your feelings first, then think about what you feel.

You need plenty of time to take in and respond to information.

You're influenced by your peer group; you like participation and collaboration.

You strive for personal understanding and empathy.

You need a sense of social harmony.

Your philosophy is: "Be cautious and make sure it works for everyone."

Learning Style Two: Truthkeeper

You learn best if allowed to concentrate on one topic until thoroughly understood.

You need thoroughly detailed instructions and documentation.

You prefer working alone.

You like time to think things through completely step by step before talking.

You process information intellectually rather than emotionally.

You prefer getting data from reading and lectures.

You value carefully documented evidence.

You reject subjective judgment and appreciate intellectual achievement.

You need a sense of personal control.

Your philosophy is: "It's valid if logical and fits with what I know."

Learning Style Three: Solutionseeker

You enjoy making decisions and solving problems.

You are matter-of-fact and bottom-line oriented.

You take the first opportunity to apply new ideas to practical situations.

You like to work independently and can work well from clear instructions.

You prefer getting information through hands-on experiences.

You like being in charge of your own learning.

You discount information you can't use.

You process information according to its practical applications.

You need a sense of personal usefulness.

Your philosophy is: "If it works, do it."

Learning Style Four: Risktaker

You socialize easily and learn by interacting with others.

You take risks and enjoy challenges and change.

You do best when you're learning with other high-energy people.

You prefer looking at information from many viewpoints as you learn.

You're in love with "newness" i.e. new ideas, activities, experiences.

You enjoy shifting back and forth between topics or activities.

You like to develop your own way of doing things.

You see the big picture and future possibilities.

You need a sense of personal excitement.

Your philosophy is: "I'll try anything once."

---

2. **Think you can create a doodle representing each learning style?** Come on, live dangerously! Grab some colored pens and draw four doodles in the following box, one for each style. The doodles will capture the essence of the styles as you understand them. If you want to try an interesting experiment, teach someone else what you know about learning styles and have that person draw four doodles too. Then compare your doodles and explain them to each other. You'll be surprised at the similarities and contrasts you'll see emerge and at the depth of your own understanding as you share what you know about styles.

3. **The single most important variable in determining where you park your car (how you learn) is:**

A. *available parking space*

B. *what you're doing at the time you're doing it (i.e. the task at hand)*

C. *where you're told to park your car*

D. *where you feel like parking your car*

How did you do?

For A: Gotcha!

For B: Right on!

For C and D: Sometimes you learn in certain ways because you're told to do it that way or because you feel like doing it that way. The major factor in deciding how to learn, however, is what you're doing at the time.

4. Put a star (check mark is okay too) beside the four most important facts to remember about learning styles:

A. *There are four major ways of learning and it's helpful to remember the characteristics of each so that you can recognize your students' preferred learning styles.*

B. *Fun stuff, this styles information, but really irrelevant in your day-to-day work, and pretty impractical besides.*

C. *Learning styles form the foundation of successful instruction; teaching to all ways of learning is the major goal in using the styles information.*

D. *You now have a reason to say, "I don't do it that way because I'm a One, (or Two Three, Four)."*

E. *You learn in all four ways and you have your own personal blend of all four styles.*

F. *Learning styles have nothing to do with the ways you give information to others.*

G. *The way you learn best is the best way for everyone else to learn.*

H. *The styles map is based on the needs of all four types of learners and automatically honors the learning diversity of your students.*

Check your answers:

For A, C, E, H: You got 'em! Well done!

For B, D, F, G: You might want to go back and reread the chapter. Then again, you might want to stop here and take a long break. Come back when you're rested and try again.

5. In the space below, write the reactions to the styles information expressed by the two people you shared the information with.

6. Which style(s) did you highlight the most? The least?

7. Does your preferred style(s) in these lists match those you marked in the chapter?

8. List three of your most positive learning strengths:

Chapter Four:
Reset Your Compass Often.

Chapter Four:
Reset Your Compass Often.

· · · · ·

It was a clear spring day, light winds, and I was attempting my second cross-country flight, this time from South Lake Tahoe to Chico, California, about two-hundred miles north one way (by car). I was very proud of myself because I was *NOT* following the roads, my navigation was right-on, and my Chico landing was A+ (Gary would have been proud too). Anyway, I landed, taxied, radioed the control tower that I was ready to take off again, received permission to do so, and resumed flying, feeling very, very good. You can imagine my bewilderment when the control tower radioed me with a question, *"Cessna 4410-Romeo, what did you say your destination was?"* When I replied *"South Lake Tahoe,"* silence filled the airwaves. Then the control tower observed thoughtfully, *"You must be a student pilot. I can help you. In order to get to South Lake Tahoe, you need to fly south, not north!"* An embarrassed pause followed as I realized that I was indeed flying the opposite direction of my flight plan. The tower offered me an excuse by stating kindly, *"We understand. You just forgot to reset your compass, didn't you?"* Yup, I had forgotten to reset the card compass, one of two compasses in a Cessna 172. It is the compass that you need to reset often in order to stay on course.

Using the learning styles information while teaching is like resetting your compass – you're always checking to see if you're on course and if you're addressing the learning needs of your students. *Resetting your compass means constantly monitoring and adjusting the learning activities and direction of your teaching so that the four learning styles are honored.*

Resetting your compass is also called "style-stretching." Style-stretching refers to using other ways of giving information that may not be the ones you're the most comfortable with.

> **Style-stretching means**
> **varying the ways you give information**
> **to make sure that all your learners get it.**

But before you can begin to reset your compass, you need to know what your learning style behaviors look like when you're teaching a class or conducting a training from a specific style corner. **How DOES your particular learning preference influence the ways you teach?**

Here are some descriptions of how you might think, feel, and what your personal goals may be when you're instructing others. Highlight the one(s) that best describe you.

1. If you're a strong Style One, connecting and bonding with your learners is very important to you – and you want them to connect with each other also. You want the ambience of the learning environment to be pleasing and nurturing. You tend to avoid any form of conflict. You'll often let your students take the lead, adjusting your content to fit their needs. You seek to establish peaceful and harmonious learning experiences.

2. If you're a strong Style Two, accurate information presented in a logical, sequential manner is of the utmost importance. You focus on the material, making sure it is thorough and factual. You are uncomfortable with interactive situations over which you have no control. You plan your work and work your plan. You seek to establish a sound basis of knowledge.

3. If you're a strong Style Three, the most important factor to you is personal usefulness. You want your students to walk away with skills they can use, practical stuff that works for them. You tend to avoid what you see as "time-wasting" activities such as group discussions and feeling-centered experiences. You seek to establish real-life application of the information learned.

4. If you're a strong Style Four, high-energy activities that challenge your learners are important to you. You want them to step out of the old ways of doing things and embrace new ideas, new risks, new attitudes, new beliefs. You are uncomfortable with details and routine, preferring to reinvent learning procedures as you go. You seek to energize and motivate your students to take charge of their own learning.

Obviously, then, your teaching goals will differ depending upon which style strength you're emphasizing. Of course you may have goals that span more than one style. *The ideal is to have a goal or series of goals that meet the needs of all four styles.*

I said earlier that **the ways you take in information (learn) usually affect the ways you give out information (teach, train, communicate).** For example, if you learn best by talking about information with others, you'll probably allow for many periods of dialogue among students. If you like challenges and risk when you learn, you'll most likely design a class or training to include competition or the challenge of a difficult task. If you learn by reading and listening to a lecture, you'll probably assume that most people learn the way you do and therefore you'll expect your students to do the same. If you learn through hands-on experiences, you'll minimize lecture and maximize how-to-do-it type activities. When you park your car in your favorite spot, you'll usually choose teaching methods which will indicate your style preference.

Having said that, I need to point out that sometimes the opposite occurs. Your teaching style may, in fact, be different from your learning style. When that happens, ask yourself, "Why?" It may be you already know that always teaching in the ways you learn best doesn't work for many of your students. So you've learned to use a variety of teaching strategies to reach all your students. Or maybe the system in which you teach encourages you to use certain instructional methods while discouraging you from using others. It's safe to say, though, that ***more often you'll find yourself instructing others in ways you like to be instructed.***

Here are some instructional strategies you probably use when you're teaching from a One, Two, Three, or Four parking place:

1. *As a One, you often include activities that will help your students get to know each other.* You like time for discussion and processing various learning activities, time to think about what is being learned, and time to express feelings. You tend to use collaborative learning methods such as small groups and pairs. Your students' needs will often lead you to change your plans. You may have a slower, more laid-back delivery style.

2. *As a Two, you tend to emphasize the material presented with lecture, note-taking, handouts, and reading formats.* Quite often the major portion of a learning situation will involve your students listening while you explain the information presented. Dialogue will usually be question and answer or one person talking at a time. You may have a very businesslike, step-by-step, factual delivery style.

3. As a Three, your lecture and handouts will reflect your commitment to the bottom line – the usefulness and practicality of what is being taught. If there is a skill to be learned, you usually demonstrate it during the lesson. You often use a lecture format to give concrete real-life examples of what you're teaching. You may have a very fast and to-the-point delivery style.

4. As a Four, you tend to use your energy and enthusiasm to engage your students in activities and dialogue. You enjoy entertaining while you teach so you will often "birdwalk," i.e. tell stories that indirectly relate to the subject. You may use a variety of unique activities during the lesson. You usually have a high-energy, dramatic delivery style.

Once you understand the goals you hold and the behaviors you show when you're acting from your preferred place, you can begin consciously to "stretch" to other parking places. Resetting your compass or "style-stretching." is simply moving from one style to another so that your compass doesn't stay "stuck" in lecture mode, in dialogue mode, in the telling stories mode, or wherever you're most comfortable. **With style-stretching, you make sure you're using a variety of teaching methods to present your material so that your students can learn in a number of different ways.**

Style-stretching also keeps you from doing over and over what doesn't work for many of your learners.

Many times I've watched teachers and trainers who, when it's obvious to them that their learners are lost, repeat the same information in the same way, only louder and faster. Deborah Tannen calls this *"complementary schismogenesis – the spiraling effect of trying harder by applying more of the same style."* Another way of putting it is the tongue-in-cheek definition of insanity: *doing the same thing over and over again but expecting different results.*

Speaking of insanity, there IS a downside to each style. **Knowing what your "poorly-managed" side looks like can help you "reset your compass," in this case recognize and change the negative traits.** Actually, if you take your positive characteristics and exaggerate them, you'll most likely bump up against some negative qualities. **It's a matter of DEGREE more than anything – the degree to which you behave one way can move you into a negative place.** For example, a Four's spontaneous ability to go-with-the-flow can lead to an inability to adequately meet the goals of the class or training. A Two's ability to focus on facts may stifle the humor and fun that is necessary for successful learning. Threes may use their gift of problem-solving to solve everybody else's problems without allowing the learners time to figure it out themselves. And Ones may take their sensitivity to an extreme and feel personally attacked when questioned by a skeptic in the class.

In other words, the poorly-managed traits are simply the opposite sides of the positively-managed coins.

Here are more examples of what some poorly-managed teaching behaviors might look like.

1. A poorly-managed One may seem too soft-spoken, slow, and wishy-washy in his teaching. Wanting to be liked may take precedence over positive group management. Peace at any price may stifle the learning that comes from the initial clash of conflicting opinions and beliefs. He may get lost in feelings to the detriment of the learning.

2. A poorly-managed Two may seem too rigid and controlling in her teaching. The material and the lesson plan may get more attention than the students. Wanting it to be perfect (and wanting to be right) may take precedence over allowing the human elements of dialogue and movement to flow. She may delve into analysis so completely that the larger goal of the learning is lost.

3. A poorly-managed Three may seem too pushy and opinionated in her teaching. The "my way or the highway" approach may alienate many students. Sometimes there may appear to be a total disregard for the feelings and opinions of others and the students' need for time to process the material. She may move to action so quickly that data is lost and mistakes are made.

4. A poorly-managed Four may seem too flighty and scattered in his teaching. Entertainment may take precedence over learning. A propensity for nonstop talking, however funny it may be, may use up all the learning time. He can get fragmented and out-of-touch with the learning goals.

So you've recognized a few teaching behaviors with which you're not especially pleased. That's a great first step! Awareness of your downside helps you move away from the *"I taught it but they didn't learn it,"* or the *"Why can't they get it? It's so easy to understand,"* or the *"If they'd just do what I tell them, they'd get it,"* mentalities.

A birdwalk: Sue Channel, a gifted high school math teacher, wanted me to remind you of the old maxim: *"You can lead a horse to water but you can't make him drink"* – i.e. on occasion you WILL encounter a student who simply refuses to learn the presented material, *and his reasons for doing so have NOTHING to do with you or the learning experience.* What to do? Take a deep breath, know that you've done all you can do to create a lesson or training which works for most of your learners, let go of expectations, and allow the student to experience the natural consequences of his choice. The bottom line? ***Learning is a conscious choice and one that can't be forced.*** All we can do as teachers and trainers is to create optimum learning environments for our students. One of the ways to do this is to make sure we use a variety of teaching methods to reach all learning styles.

"Okay," you say, *"How DO I learn to stretch out of my comfort zone and try some other not-so-comfortable teaching techniques?"*

Here are a few quick suggestions which illustrate how simple style-stretching can be:

1. If your strength is Oneness, set a time-limit for each interactive portion of your lesson and stick to it. Rehearse your delivery beforehand until you can present it in a somewhat quicker, more assertive way. During the lesson, practice paraphrasing dissenting opinions rather than trying to make everyone agree with each other. Learn to state what *YOU* really believe and not what you think *THEY* want to hear. Make sure you include some individual work time as well as group time. Learn to let it be okay if some of your students don't like you.

2. If your strength is Twoness, allow your students time to ask questions and to share their own knowledge, opinions, and feelings about what you're teaching them. Include in your lecture stories and metaphors which illuminate your points. Use cartoons and other visuals on charts and overhead transparencies while you talk. Take baby-steps towards relaxing your adherence to the schedule and the lesson plan. Smile – and learn not to take yourself or your topic so seriously!

3. If your strength is Threeness, you also need to give your students time to discuss, question, and elaborate on the material you're presenting. In addition, paraphrasing their comments indicates that you really heard what they had to say and that their opinions are valued (even if you don't think they're right). Allow time at the beginning of your lesson for the students to get to know each other. Wait at least five seconds after you ask *ANY* question before you jump in with the answer. Practice the "three-before-me" rule: elicit three comments from your students before you give your opinion on the subject being discussed.

4. If your strength is Fourness, it's imperative that you, too, stick to a time-limit for each section of your lesson – in fact, assign a timekeeper from the group to keep you on track. Devise a way of sticking to your agenda that works for you. Jan Thurman, a gifted counselor and trainer, uses brightly-colored little post-it notes which she sticks to a chart agenda. As she covers the points on the post-it notes, she removes them one-at-a-time from the chart. That way she knows that she has covered the material in a sequential way – and it still gives her the freedom to embellish her material with stories and humorous anecdotes.

Another great style-stretching idea comes from **Presenting with Pizzazz:**

Balance active and passive ways of learning.

In others words, follow a sit-down-and-listen lecture with a stand-up-and-move-around activity. Include a quiet thinking activity in between two talking activities. Follow a writing time with a discussion time. For every ten minutes of lecture, include a one-minute *Pair Share* activity (by the end of this book, you'll know what that is). This balancing act automatically helps you vary your teaching methods.

By the way, one of the all-time best ways to learn how to stretch to other teaching styles is to hang

out with someone who parks his car in that place. Find a teaching or training buddy who is most comfortable in the style corner that's most uncomfortable for you. Pick his brain, or better yet, team-teach with him for awhile. Or find a number of friends who all have different style preferences and use each other as resources.

What about your students? How about *THEIR* poorly-managed style traits? What do *THEIR* learning style behaviors look like? Hmm, very similar to yours:

1. *Strong Style One students want to please you.* They learn best when they have a friendly relationship with you and the other students. They need to talk things over and time to take it all in. They'll seem a little more passive than the other styles and tend to be quiet at first until they feel comfortable in the learning situation. If they feel psychologically threatened in a learning experience, their poorly-managed behaviors appear and they'll withdraw into silence, act in very indirect ways to show displeasure, or take on the role of "helpless victim" who feels powerless to change things.

2. *Strong Style Two students want to get good grades and know the right answers.* They thrive on rules and routine. They need information presented in a logical manner and quiet time to think things through. They may feel uneasy about joining in a discussion or group activity until they know why it's important to the learning. They actually prefer to work alone. If they feel psychologically threatened in a class or training, their poorly-managed side takes over and they become overly critical and judgmental of the teacher, the other students, the subject-matter, and sometimes of themselves. They too will use indirect ways to show displeasure. Side-comments and sarcasm are two of these.

3. *Strong Style Three students want lots of hands-on learning with minimal instruction from you.* They

learn best when their bodies have something to do besides listening. They need to know the outcome and
"bottom-line" of an activity before they'll feel comfortable joining in. They would rather figure things out by
themselves at first and then they'll work as part of a
group, especially if they can be the leader. If they feel
psychologically threatened in a learning situation, you'll
know it because they'll act out what they feel in very
direct ways – loud comments, abrasive actions, the *"I
hate this and I'm outa here"* type of poorly-managed be-
havior.

**4. Strong Style Four students want fun, high-energy
learning experiences that hold their interest.** They
learn best when you give them challenges and surprises,
then get out of their way. Like the Ones, they love
interaction, especially with other students who are high-
energy people like them. The more the merrier. Once they
know what the "big picture" is, they'll do anything with
enthusiasm, provided it doesn't bore them. When
psychologically threatened in a class or training, they
can become very dramatic, or they'll go off into their own
world and entertain themselves. Another poorly-managed
trait of Fours is to use humor as a weapon – becoming
the class clown who interrupts all the time and makes
jokes about everything.

By now you're asking, *"How in the world do I get to
know each of my student's learning styles? How do
I stretch to each of the style places to meet all their
learning needs? How do I do it ALL?"*

**So here's the sensational secret about style-
stretching:** Once you finish reading this book and
begin using the powerfully effective styles map, you
won't have to worry about style-stretching, resetting your compass, or where you park your car.
Why? Because the map does it all for you. **With
the styles map as your guide, you'll meet most
of the learning needs of your students most of
the time.** Furthermore, following the map means

you'll seldom move into a poorly-managed place, and you'll automatically stretch as you deliver your lesson or training. In fact, you'll do it so naturally that you'll be amazed you could ever teach anyone anything without it.

> *The most powerful individuals...*
> *will be those who do the best job*
> *of transferring knowledge to others.*
> *...Bob Buckman*

> *There is no such thing*
> *as teaching without learning.*
> *If they haven't learned it,*
> *you haven't taught it.*
> *...Benna Kallik*

> *Unless you move,*
> *the place where you are*
> *is the place where you'll always be.*
> *...Ashleigh Brilliant*

Ground School

$\bullet\ \bullet\ \bullet\ \bullet\ \bullet$

1. **You're just about ready to start conducting a new training. As you take care of the last minute details (Is there a long enough extension cord? Are all the handout materials on the table?) you notice four participants enter the room one at a time. Suddenly it seems as if you're blessed with magical powers: you realize you can read their thoughts. You do a little mental eavesdropping and figure out their preferred learning styles (label each of the following with a style number):**

A. *"Place looks interesting. Some posters on the walls and a cartoon on the overhead. Sure hope this trainer isn't boring. Looks like a fun group of people. Wonder if it'll be entertaining enough for me to stick around for the whole day. If not, I'm outa here. Think I'll introduce myself to the trainer while I'm waiting and let her know who I am."*

B. *"I think this is the right room. Wonder where I'm supposed to sit. Maybe I'll just stand in the back here until I see what the other people are doing. I hope I don't have to embarrass myself by getting up in front of people and introducing myself. Wouldn't mind knowing who the other people in the room are though. I'll sit beside someone who seems friendly. The trainer looks like a nice person. Sure hope I feel comfortable here."*

C. *"Let's see, there's the table with name tags and handout materials. Better make sure I don't miss getting the things I need for the training. Good, there's an agenda so I know what's going to be* covered. *Wonder what the trainer's credentials are. I'll sit over here where I can take notes and not be bothered by other people."*

D. *"This better be good. I need some hard and fast ideas that really work. Sure hope the trainer doesn't do any of that touchy-feely stuff like having us introduce ourselves and get to know each other – it wastes my time. If I get a few good ideas I can use I'll consider this training worthwhile. I'll sit by the door where I can make a quick escape if necessary."*

Check out who they are:

A *is a Style Four learner.*

B *is a Style One learner.*

C *is a Style Two learner.*

D *is a Style Three learner.*

2. You're walking through a community college hallway as four instructors in four different classrooms are almost ready to begin their lessons. Again, you suddenly realize you can hear their thoughts. You listen in (label each of the following with a styles number):

A. *"Yup, everything's ready – desks here and breakout area there for the activities I'll be leading. I've got about five minutes to make sure the students sit where I want them to sit for the beginning of the class. We have a lot to cover so there'll be no dillydallying – they've got to be ready to begin on time."*

B. *"This is going to be so much fun. Look at the interesting students who just walked in. Better introduce myself and let them know how much* they're going to enjoy the class. Think I have most of the details taken care of – can't remember where I put my list. Oh, well, I'll wing it if I've forgotten anything."

C. "I'm a little nervous but I know that'll pass once I get started. Those students over there seem friendly. Hope they like me. Maybe I should introduce myself and find out who they are and why they're here. That way I'll have a better idea as to what their expectations are. I want everyone to get along and have a good time together while they learn."

D. "Extension cord, spare overhead projector bulb, handouts, felt pens ... yes, I've got everything checked off on my list. Looks like nothing's been left out. I have five minutes to look over my notes before I begin. As long as there aren't any interruptions I can keep to my schedule. Room looks organized. Everything's in place. Good. I'm ready."

Check your answers against these:

A is a *Style Three* instructor.

B is a *Style Four* instructor.

C is a *Style One* instructor.

D is a *Style Two* instructor.

3. **Now it's your turn to teach someone else something about learning styles. Call a buddy and tell her three facts about each style. Ask her to share what she knows about styles. In the margins on this page, write your thoughts and insights.**

Chapter Five:
The Map Is Not
The Territory.

Chapter Five:
The Map Is Not
The Territory.

· · · · ·

When I was eight years old, I flew in a commercial airplane for the first time. Until then, my only view of the United States from the air had been the geographical maps found in my mother's atlas and the textbooks at school. I felt excited and also a little smug. Even though I had never flown before, I knew what I would see as we flew over various states: I would see the black lines separating one state from another so that the passengers would know where they were as they moved across the country. I craned my neck to look for those lines and my anxiety grew as the plane's captain announced that we were passing Four Corners where four states touch each other, and all I saw was brown desert everywhere. I searched futilely for those lines, and at some point disappointedly realized that they only existed on the maps, not on the earth itself.

I tell you that story because, a lifetime later when I was learning to fly as the pilot instead of the passenger – and using those aeronautical charts I mentioned – I discovered that the sectionals were crisscrossed with blue lines which represented "sky roads," as I called them – highways in the sky for airplanes to follow. Not unlike the black state lines, the eight-year old part of me secretly looked for the blue lines in the air.

In her book **That's Not What I Meant,** Deborah Tannen cautions:

"The map is not the territory."

A road map represents the territory you're driving through, but it isn't the real territory at all. The same applies to aeronautical charts. And the same can be said for the styles map. **The map is simply your flight plan to help make the learning stick.** Furthermore, all the educational, medical, and psychological research that went into creating the map is like those blue lines on the aeronautical chart – invisible in real life. The research is the behind-the-scenes stuff that helps you create the learning experience. Whether you're in front of a class of students or a roomful of business people, it's the territory, i.e. the actual learning experience, that counts.

By the way, the styles map in this book is my adaptation of that research. My slant. My understanding. What works for me. You take my take (so to speak) and make it your own. **You blend your own artistry and energy as a giver of knowledge with the workings of the map and bingo – a new learning experience is born!**

Finally, there is nothing sacred about the map. It's not set in cement. You aren't violating any secret code if you change it to fit your own needs and those of your learners. I hereby give you carte-blanche permission to play with the steps, change their order, flip-flop back and forth between steps, and experiment with what works best for you. I will urge you, though, first to become comfortable with the steps in the order they're presented before you begin to make your own maps. It's a smart thing to do to familiarize yourself with the best and quickest route to a new destination before you scout out the back roads and alternative routes, **Similarly, using the styles map steps in numerical order at first will give you the practice you need before you begin to change the pieces around.**

In flying jargon, we've done the run-up and it's time for the takeoff. Here's a birds-eye view of the four "roads" (steps or pieces) of the styles map. I've created a phrase for each piece to help you remember all four:

Step #1: **Getting Connected**
Step #2: **Sharing The Wealth**
Step #3: **Making It Happen**
Step #4: **Celebrating Success**

Each step in the map meets the needs of one particular learning style. **In other words, the four steps of the map correspond to the four major ways people learn.** When you have all four pieces present in your lesson or training, you're meeting the learning needs of all four learning styles. The map helps you design a learning experience which works for most people most of the time.

Here's a short description of each step:

Step #1: Getting Connected. At the beginning of the learning experience, you want your students to connect with each other as well as with what they know about the topic to be presented. You want them to feel positive about themselves, the group, and what they're about to learn. **David Meier, Director of The Center for Accelerated Learning and creator of "The Accelerated Learning Training Methods Workshop," calls this step the "Preparation" phase where you "awaken the**

minds and remove the barriers" to learning. You are, in effect, creating a "learning community" within the group so that your students feel safe with each other and so that they'll be open and excited about learning together. *Your Style One learners will feel especially comfortable during this step.*

Step #2: Sharing the Wealth. The second step in the learning experience is the one you're used to doing, the one you've spent much of your time perfecting: the "information giving" piece. The word "sharing" reminds you that giving information isn't just about "telling" your students what they need to know. Sharing means giving your students opportunities to respond to the material you've presented, to talk with others about their understanding of what they are learning and how it fits with what they already know. The "teaching," in effect, becomes more of a dialogue than a monologue. *David Meier refers to this step as the "Presentation" phase where "learners are INVOLVED with contextual learning in multisensory ways."* Asking your students to sit quietly and listen to you is only one facet of *Sharing the Wealth.* Dialogue is the other. *Your Style Two learners will feel confident during this step.*

Step #3: Making It Happen. It's time for the real-life application of the information your students have learned. Step Three is about skills – using what's been learned in practical ways that will work for them. *The "Practice" phase, according to David Meier, includes hands-on projects, games, and activities to bring the learning as close to real life as possible.* The more choices your students have of applying what they've learned to their own lives, the better. *Your Style Three learners will be highly motivated during this step.*

Step #4: Celebrating Success. The final step completes the learning journey even while it helps students explore future possibilities for using what they've just learned. **Meier calls this the "Performance" phase where "ongoing learning is given team-based support."** This support includes: students teaching each other what they've learned, students making action plans, i.e. personal commitments to use their new knowledge, and students sharing their appreciation of the entire experience. In effect, it is a time for celebration. **Your Style Four learners will shine during this step.**

Are you with me so far? Does the map make sense to you? Does it fit with what you already know about effective instructional practices? Do you already include all or parts of the map when you're giving information to others? Would you like a real-life example of how this map works? Here we go:

"Help! My Job Is Driving Me Crazy!" That's the title of the stress management workshop you've signed up to take because sometimes you feel like you're stressing to the max and you'd like to change that. You find a seat in the large, well-lit training room where chairs are arranged in rows in the front half of the room and the back half is empty for breakout activities. The room begins to fill with people. You settle down in your chair expecting to sit and listen for about two hours. You hope you'll learn something useful.

The trainer explains the four steps of the styles map and how they meet the needs of the four learning styles represented in the room. She indicates that the stress management workshop will follow the map. Then she begins:

#1 Getting Connected. The trainer directs you and the rest of the participants to stand up and move around the room mumbling under your breath *"Relax, relax, relax relax."* When she says "stop" you form a standing group with three or four of the people you're standing closest to. You shake hands, introduce yourselves to each other and answer the questions the trainer has posted on a chart: *"What is one situation that really pushes your buttons? What do you do about it when it happens? What would you like to learn from this workshop?"* The trainer gives you a few minutes to chat, then asks for some volunteers to share their answers with the whole group. She thanks you and you return to your seat. *(Can you see how she has connected you to the other people in the group as well as to your own stressors, stress reactions, and personal goals for the workshop? You have begun to form a "learning community" for the duration of the workshop.)*

#2 Sharing The Wealth. The trainer leads you through a short "guided imagery" (imagination) activity which shows you how powerful your own mind-body connection is. Then with pictures and cartoons displayed on the overhead projector, she illustrates what your brain does when you're stressing out. You fill out a note-taking page as she talks. When she finishes, you turn to your neighbor and share the most important thing you learned from her mini-lecture. *(Did you notice that you were actively involved during the lecture, first with the guided imagery activity, then with your attention to the cartoons and note-taking, and finally reviewing the information verbally with a partner?)*

#3 Making It Happen. Now the trainer has you move to the empty break-out area in the back of the room. She leads the large group in a number of standing and moving physical exercises which help reduce the negative effects of stress. You also experience ways to clear your mind and calm your body. A large group discussion follows as you and the other participants brainstorm your own stress management techniques. *(You've begun to practice practical skills you can use in your own*

*life and you've also learned some more useful infor-
mation from the other participants.)*

#4 Celebrating Success. The trainer divides the whole
group into small groups of four to six people. In your
small group, you design a stress-management activity
which will involve the whole group. Each small group
takes turns demonstrating and teaching its activity. Afterwards, groups applaud each other. The trainer gives
you some more information about available resources
(people, books, tapes, trainings) which will help you create a more stress-free life. Finally, she ends with a closing activity where you stand and find new partners with
whom to share your answers to the following questions:
*"What is the most important thing you learned in the past
two hours? What is one thing you promise yourself that
you're going to do with what you've learned? What is one
thing you can share with someone else at work or at home
about what you've learned and who is the person you're
going to share it with?"* You walk out the door feeling
good about what you've learned, feeling close to the people
you just spent the last 120 minutes with, and knowing
that you can indeed do one or two really practical things
to get started in a new stress-free direction. *(You've
taught each other some new skills, celebrated the
journey with activities and applause, and made a
commitment to use the new information in practical ways.)*

Did this short example help you see how simple and
practical the styles map is in designing effective learning experiences? Did you notice how much richer
the two hours seemed than if the trainer had just
lectured on stress management for 120 minutes?
Was it easy to recognize the relationship between
the four steps of the map and the different needs of
the four basic learning styles? Can you use some of
these learning activities in your own work?

Bob Pike, in his **Creative Training Techniques
Handbook,** has coined a wonderful phrase to cap-

ture the essence of the type of learning experience the map creates:

Instructor-led, participant-centered.

He elaborates: *"It focuses as many of the learning activities as possible on the participants themselves. Sure it requires some thought and creativity, but it can be a powerful learning tool that produces positive results."*

That's fine, you say, if you're instructing a group of people. But what about a one-on-one situation? Like showing a co-worker a new procedure? Or instructing your own child? Or helping a friend learn something?

Let's revisit the map, only this time you're teaching a co-worker how to use a new software program. One-on-one. You, your colleague, and the computer.

#1 Getting Connected. You ask your co-worker to tell you what her experience has been with computers in general and this particular software program in particular. You listen, ask questions, and paraphrase what she's said so she knows you understand where she's coming from. Doing this also helps her clarify what she knows and doesn't know. *She now feels connected to you, connected to her own knowledge and feelings about the software, and comfortable in the learning experience.*

#2 Sharing the Wealth. You give her an overview of the important features of the software program. You ask her to repeat some of the information, or you ask her questions about what you've told her. That way, she gets to talk about it, figure out how much she's understood, and ask you questions if she's not clear on certain points. She's an active part of this step as she talks about what she's learned so far. *You have both participated in an* *exchange of information even as you gave her new knowledge to work with.*

#3 Making it Happen. Now, with your guidance, she sits at the computer and works through the steps of the software program. *HER* hands are on the keyboard, not yours! You're simply the "guide-on-the-side" who helps her with any difficult pieces. *She spends some time using the software, practicing, making adjustments, learning through doing.*

#4 Celebrating Success. Finally, you ask her to teach you what she's learned. By doing this, she reviews the information and you can correct any misunderstandings. You have her tell you how she plans to use the software program, and you compliment her for her efforts. Both of you might even go out for coffee to celebrate her achievement! *She knows what she's learned, she's made a commitment to use the software, she feels good about the whole learning experience.*

Can you see how easily the styles map can be adapted to one-on-one learning experiences? Yes, it takes more time this way than simply telling somebody something and hoping they got it. But if you count the times you've had to repeat, reteach, retrain, or straighten out someone's mistakes because he didn't learn it well in the first place, you actually save time in the long run.

Now you ask, *"But what about a classroom situation where I have the same group of students everyday?"*

Here's one more example: Let's say you're teaching a high school English literature class and the subject is **Romeo and Juliet.**

#1 Getting Connected. Before beginning the unit on **Romeo and Juliet,** *you decide upon a theme which will*

connect your students' lives to the Shakespeare play. The theme might be love, hatred, prejudice, family feuds, whatever is meaningful to you and your students. You may create an activity that gets your students involved in the theme or you may simply have them discuss their own experiences related to the theme. **You're connecting your students to each other and to a theme which will link the literature to their own lives.**

#2 Sharing the Wealth. You give students information pertaining to the play as well as to the theme you've chosen: background history, language and customs of the period, etc. You do this through lecture, visuals, movie clips, note-taking, worksheets, discussion groups, and other ways of involving your students as you teach them. **Your students are actively involved in their own learning.**

#3 Making it Happen: You may move back and forth between Step Two and Step Three as you have your students read and act out various parts of the play itself. In addition, you may have them create modern day reenactments of certain scenes to be presented in Step Four. Or they may create advertising posters for the play. Or they may compare the movie versions of **Romeo and Juliet** and **Westside Story.** And they can hunt for more cultural examples of the theme from the beginning of the unit. **Your students now use the information they've learned in a number of hands-on ways.**

#4 Celebrating Success. Students may present their reenactments for the class or school. They may make displays of their posters or other projects. They may create a small Shakespeare fair for the community. They can also discuss what they've learned and how it all relates to their own lives outside the classroom experience. **Your students are involved in ways of bringing what they've learned into their own lives and the lives of the school and community. Their lives have been enriched by what they've done with what they've learned.**

The styles map builds connections, understanding, skills, and possibilities for your learners. It meets the needs of all four learning preferences. It enhances long-term learning. It makes the learning experience a success for most students and shows them how to do productive things with what they've learned.

To summarize it all, the styles map is the key to teaching anyone anything and making it stick. So tighten your seat belt! In the next few chapters we're going to zoom in for a closer look at each of the four steps of this simple but effective flight plan.

> ***We don't receive wisdom;***
> ***we must discover it for ourselves***
> ***after a journey that no one can take for us***
> ***or spare us from.***
> *...Marcel Proust*

> ***If you don't know where you're going,***
> ***you might end up somewhere else.***
> *...Anonymous*

> ***Education has so much to learn!***
> *...Ashleigh Brilliant*

Ground School

• • • • •

1. What is the most important thing to remember about the styles map?

A. *It's a useful metaphor for how we give and receive information.*

B. *It reminds us that the traditional classroom-style lecture methods never really worked that well anyway.*

C. *You will need to use it the next time you're flying an airplane.*

D. *Its sequential steps are designed to meet the needs of all four learning styles.*

And now for the answer envelope:

For A: It is indeed, but this isn't the most important thing to remember.

For B: True, but not of utmost importance.

For C: Wrong map!

For D: Go Edsel!

2. The first step in the map focuses on:

A. *connecting your learners to each other and to the topic of the learning experience.*

B. *"breaking the ice" and using a fun opening activity.*

C. *connecting your students to your ideas and personality.*

D. *spending a lot of time building trust and getting to know each other.*

Check your own:

For A: You're a whiz at this!

For B: Icebreakers and fun opening activities are only effective for all learning styles when they connect students to the topic as well as to each other.

For C: I've watched teachers and trainers do this time and time again (and have been guilty of it myself) – telling stories, personal anecdotes, and entertaining the learners so that they know who the teacher or trainer is but they don't know each other at all. I'm not discounting the entertainment and educational value of a snazzy opening story – it's just not enough when doing Step One.

For D: Although getting to know each other IS a part of Step One, you don't have to spend a lot of time doing it. While connecting people to people and people to content, your opening activities can be short and simple, yet very effective, Remember, just getting to know each other isn't enough.

3. What is the primary goal of Step Two?

A. *You lecture to your students while they listen to what you have to say.*

B. *Your students now teach each other about the topic.*

C. *Every person takes out his pocket change and "shares the wealth" with everyone else (I couldn't resist that one!).*

D. *You create ways to give and receive information that involve your students.*

And the answers:

For A or B: These are parts of Step Two but they aren't the primary goal.

For D: Outa sight!

4. In Step Three:

A. *you tell your students how to use the information presented in Step Two.*

B. *you turn your learners loose to do whatever they want with the information they've learned.*

C. *you design activities which will help your students practice skills related to the topic.*

D. *you become the "guide-on-the-side" as your learners practice using the content in practical ways.*

Check them puppies:

For A: Nope! Try again.

For B: Your learners still need your guidance at this point to help them use what they've just learned in Step Two. So you'll design activities which will encourage them to apply their new skills with your assistance if necessary.

For C and D: Hot dog – both answers are correct!

5. What is the main purpose of Step Four?

A. *Your students make a commitment to use what they've learned and they celebrate the learning journey they've shared together.*

B. *You create fun closing activities so that your learners leave on an "energy high."*

C. *Your students teach each other what they've learned and decide how to use their new skills in real-life situations.*

D. *This is the time to give your learners more information concerning the topic before they leave.*

A final check:

For A and C: You're on a roll – both answers are valid goals for Step Four.

If you chose B or D: "Energy highs" are a by-product of Step Four, not the primary goal itself. As for giving more information on the topic before they leave, I always use a bit of Step Four time to give my learners other resources (books titles, trainings, classes, people, organization names, etc.) concerning the topic just covered. I also include a final question-answer time to address any last-minute questions or concerns. Even with this, the main goal of Step Four is NOT the delivery of more information related to the topic.

Chapter Six:
Getting Connected.

Chapter Six:
Getting Connected.

• • • • •

Time travel again! Like the movie "Groundhog Day," you've suddenly been transported back in time to a familiar scene you've just experienced: the two hour stress management seminar (in the last chapter) that you signed up to take. Once again you find yourself walking towards the training room hoping to learn something useful. As you set foot inside the door several very interesting things are going on inside your head, things you may not even be aware of.

The most immediate thing you do automatically and unconsciously is to check out the physical surroundings to make sure that you'll be physically "safe." *The survival part of your brain (also called the subcortex or reptilian brain) is registering comfort or discomfort.* Are you hungry or thirsty? Are the chairs comfortable or uncomfortable? Is there room to move around or do you feel closed in? Is the room too hot or too cold? (I once held a workshop in a room where the temperature was about ten degrees too hot and couldn't be controlled – the participants couldn't move past survival brain. They stayed focused on how uncomfortable they were and very little learning took place the entire day.) All this survival brain stuff takes a matter of seconds. Ah, you decide all is well; your physical comfort is assured. You relax a little and your brain does a quick shift.

Now you check out how you feel emotionally. A little anxious? Nervous maybe? Watchful? On guard? Do you know the instructor? How about the other participants? Do you feel comfortable being around them? Will you be asked to do something that might embarrass you, like answering a question when you're not ready to? Is there a chance you might make a fool of yourself? **Your emotional (limbic) brain is determining your psychological safety in this situation.** After you do the "Relax, relax" opening activity (the one where you moved around and chatted with the other participants about your own stress reactions), your emotional brain decides that you'll be fine. *"Yup. Seems like a nice group of people. Think I like the instructor. Everything feels okay. Glad that I'm here."* This limbic brain stuff may take a few minutes to move through. When finished checking out your emotional comfort, your brain does one final shift.

Your thinking brain – the gray matter that can do its job effectively only after being assured that your physical and psychological safety are no longer problems. Now you can relax and learn. You're eager to see what's next. **Your thinking brain (cerebrum or neocortex) moves into high gear as you get ready to absorb as much new information as you can.** And so you participate in the stress management seminar with gusto, learning and enjoying it all.

When you feel safe, you're open to new experiences, new ideas, new ways of doing things. When you don't feel safe, you spend most of your time defending your own beliefs and opinions, putting up roadblocks to new learning, clinging to the old ways: *"Yeah, that might work for you but it'll never work for me."* Or: *"I don't care what those other people think. I* *know I'm right so just give me the information I came to get and let me go home."* And you may never fully realize how important that feeling of safety is unless something happens in the learning experience to take it away. (Which is exactly what happened in the middle of a class I attended when the instructor made a sarcastic remark about a question one student had asked. For the rest of the afternoon no one else asked any questions. It wasn't psychologically safe to do so.)

The same applies to your students: when they feel safe in a learning experience, they too will be receptive to new information. And when they don't feel safe (i.e. there is *either a real or imagined* physical or psychological threat to their well-being), they'll shut down, become defensive, or show the poorly-managed style characteristics mentioned in *Chapter Four.*

One of the most important purposes for the Getting Connected step is to create a feeling of safety for your students and training participants so that they can learn without the barriers of anxiety or fear. And one of the best ways to do that is through activity and conversation.

Time to move around and talk at the beginning of a class or training is a rare gift to give your learners. Rare because it doesn't happen often and isn't the norm. Many teachers and trainers feel they have too much material to cover to allow much connecting time. So they do most if not all of the moving and talking. It may work for the teacher, but it may not be the best way to create a safe environment for the learners. And it certainly doesn't give the students permission to learn from each other.

Another thing activity and conversation enhance at the beginning of a class or training is "rapport" among learners, that illusive feeling of connection that says: *"We're all in this together."*

I love what Parker Palmer has to say about rapport. In his book ***The Company of Strangers,*** he stresses the importance of moving a group of isolated strangers to a learning "family" who will support and learn from each other during any educational experience:

> **As people act in ways**
> **which acknowledge their relatedness,**
> **they are given the abundance**
> **of (the) community itself.**

That abundance translates into learning that goes far beyond the memorization of information. Learning that you aren't alone in your perceptions. Learning that your thoughts, feelings, beliefs, and ideas have value. Learning that other people share your journey. Learning that you are indeed "safe" with these people in this experience. Palmer continues:

> **We learn that underneath**
> **all surface differences**
> **people share a common humanity ...**
> **We learn that there can –**
> **and must – be honor among strangers**
> **as well as among friends.**

Safety. Rapport. Honor among strangers as well as friends.

"But my students spend everyday together," you protest. *"We've done a lot of getting acquainted activities and they already know each other. They already feel safe with each other. They're not a bunch of strangers."* Maybe. Maybe not. Community-building doesn't happen with one activity, in one hour or

one day. You can't build a learning community on the first day of the class and then do nothing else and expect your students to remain connected for the rest of the semester. When you include connecting student to student as a necessary part of *EACH* lesson, you make sure that your learners keep those connections alive.

While researching their book **Learning Together and Alone**, David and Roger Johnson uncovered a shocking statistic:

> **The single most important indicator of incarceration as an adult is isolation as a child.**

Pretty heavy-duty thought there! Think about all the students you've seen over the years who sit silently alone, never joining in, never becoming part of the learning community in your classes. Because of that, I promise myself that each learner, no matter how shy or reluctant, will connect with at least one other person and hopefully more than one, during my class or training.

How *DO* you get your students connected to each other in meaningful ways without just chitchatting? What should they talk about so the time spent in *Step One* isn't trivialized or wasted? **More important than simple introductions is the dialogue about what they already know about the topic and what they want to learn from the class or training.**

Bob Pike in his **Creative Training Techniques Seminars,** calls this **"WIIFM,"** or **"What's In It For Me?"** He explains that students need to be given time to explore their own reasons for participating in a class or training. In effect, you're helping your learners connect with the subject you're teaching even as they get to know each other. By defining for themselves their own reasons for wanting to be there, students feel a much stronger buy-in than if you defined their reasons for them.

> *Connecting people to people*
> *and people to content*
> *through movement,*
> *dialogue, conversation:*
> *Step One of the styles map.*

Obviously, then, many "icebreakers" and "trust-building" activities must be changed so that they include connecting students to the topic being taught.

Here's an example: Let's say you're teaching a new class on budgeting and financial planning (insert any subject or topic you teach). You choose a traditional "icebreaker" which most teachers use: each student stands up and introduces himself to the others. *Now for the million dollar question: Does that introductory activity connect people to people?* (Note: passive listening is *NOT* an effective way to build a learning community.) *How about connecting people to content?* (Was *ANYTHING* mentioned about content at all?)

Now take the same introductory activity but change a few little pieces. First, you tell your students that they're going to stand up, move around the room, and introduce themselves to four other people who weren't sitting near them. They form a standing group of four and quickly answer the two questions you have posted on a chart or overhead transparency:

1. What is one experience you've had with budgeting and financial planning and how did you feel about it?

2. Why did you decide to attend this class and what do you hope to do with the new information you learn?

After the groups finish answering the questions, they return to their seats. As the instructor, you might then choose to do some "processing" or "group sharing" of answers or you might simply go on with the class. In any event, the introductory activity took no more time than the traditional introductions. In terms of learning, however, the modified activity took on a richness and depth that moved the group beyond polite and passive listening. Students were actively engaged in dialogue, community-building, and connecting with their own feelings and experiences about budgeting and financial planning. They also connected with what others felt and experienced. **In choosing to do the activity in this manner, you connected people to people and people to content in your class.** Now they're focused, relaxed, and eager to learn.

Another example: Your history class has been together all semester and you're introducing the unit on the Civil War. You have your students do an activity called *Take-A-Stand* where one side of the room stands for one issue about the war and the other side stands for the opposite issue *(example: states have the right to leave the Union whenever they wish vs. once a state is a part of the Union it has to remain a part of the Union).* Your students choose where they wish to stand on each issue. Then they talk with each other about their opinions, what they know or have heard, and their feelings about the issues. **Once again, they're connecting with each**

other as well as the content of the unit. Accuracy of information is not the focus at this point, connecting is.

How about an example really close to home? You're teaching your young son how to clean his room. First, you ask him to tell you all the reasons why he might benefit from keeping his room clean. He also tells you what he thinks "clean" means. You let him know how a clean room positively affects the entire family. *In effect, you've helped your son connect to the reasons why keeping his room clean is important for everyone.* You've done a little personal bonding with him and, at the same time, you found out exactly what he understands by the word "clean."

One final thought: YOU have to believe that it's important that your learners make these personal connections. If, in the deep recesses of your heart, you don't really feel that connections are important, you'll see the connecting activities as fluff. You might do one or two but you'll move quickly through them with little processing time afterwards, and you'll bring your students' attention back as soon as you can to yourself and the information you're giving them. *If, on the other hand, you really know that making personal connections is vitally important to the learning process, then the connecting activities will be easy for you to plan and will bring much deeper meaning in the learning for your students.*

We're back to the all important question: How DO you get your students and training participants to open up, to talk to each other, to feel safe enough to share their own thoughts, feelings, beliefs, and experiences?

Simple. You do what pilots do whenever they fly. *You create a "flight kit" which holds the necessary tools of your trade.* In the case of pilots, the flight kit is a bag which contains the necessary aeronautical charts, flight plans, flight guides, headset, charting instruments, phone numbers, etc. For your flight kit, you'll need a box, binder, manila envelope, or a real or computer-generated folder which holds a collection of activities *geared to each step of the map. You just reach into your flight kit and pull out an activity that fits the step of the styles map you're on, your teaching style, content, goals, and learners' needs.* Your flight kit is your invaluable source of ideas, activities, and materials you'll need to create your own flight plans – your own teaching maps.

Telling your students *WHY* you're having them do a particular activity – your reasons for choosing it and what you hope they get out of it – also helps them understand the importance of personal connections.

Now a special surprise for you: In gathering together the necessary ideas and activities for your own flight kit, you don't need to start from scratch! I've begun the process for you by including a beginning flight kit for each step of the map. You'll find them in the *Flight Kit* section after *Chapter Eleven.* You can add to them each time you discover another activity or idea which fits with that part of the map. Take these simple activities and tinker, mess around, play, and change them to make them your own. Make them work for *YOU.*

> *The key is to see that there are*
> *opportunities for students to learn*
> *not only about the subject in question,*
> *but also about themselves as people.*
> ...Renate Cain

If YOU'RE not connected,
THEY'RE not connected.

...Sharon Bowman

What good is a superior mind
without another superior mind
to communicate with?

...Ashleigh Brilliant

Ground School

· · · · ·

1. Mark the following true or false:

A. *In Step One, you make sure your students feel both physically and psychologically safe with you and the other students.*

B. *Getting Connected means students shake hands with everyone in the class.*

C. *You want your students to connect with each other and with the content of the class or training in Step One.*

D. *Your students will "buy in" to the learning more strongly if they first identify WHY they want to learn the content being taught.*

E. *Step One is about students practicing what they have been learning.*

F. *In Step One, students share what they already know and feel about the subject.*

G. *Any type of icebreaker will work for Step One.*

H. *Getting Connected means students will be moving and talking to each other about the content before you begin teaching them the information they came to learn.*

I. *Step One is about building a "learning community."*

Check your answers against these: T F T T F T F T T. Give yourself a pat-on-the-back if you got them all!

2. Circle the items that contain all the necessary elements of a *Getting Connected* activity:

A. *In Don's community college accounting class, students indicate how they feel about number-crunching by standing at different places in the room. Then they talk with other students about their past experiences with accounting and what they hope to learn from the class.*

B. *Charlene asks her adult trainees to take turns telling the class their names, job titles, and favorite movies (the course is about nursing practices).*

C. *Steven wants to make sure his training participants know who he is, his credentials and training experience.*

D. *In Sue's high school math class, students work together in small groups to solve an introductory math puzzle which sparks their interest in the math unit to come.*

E. *Jan asks her elementary students to share with each other what they remember from yesterday's vocabulary lesson and what they think today's new vocabulary words might mean.*

F. *Martin reviews the course syllabus, grading procedures, homework assignments, and project time lines at the beginning of his community college English class.*

Let's see how you did this time:

If you circled A, D, E, you're tops!

If you circled B, C, F, reread the chapter ASAP.

3. What is a *Flight Kit*?

A. *A box into which you put all the flying paraphernalia you own.*

B. *Your own collection of teaching and learning activities geared to the four steps of the styles map.*

C. *A bag containing emergency items for your next flight on a commercial airline.*

D. *Whatever you want it to be.*

The winner is B!

4. In the box below, draw a doodle representing your understanding of *Getting Connected*.

```



```

5. What is one way you connect your learners to each other and to the topic at the beginning of your lesson or training?

6. What is a new connecting activity you might try? (Use the *Getting Connected Flight Kit* for ideas.)

Chapter Seven:
Sharing The Wealth.

Chapter Seven:
Sharing The Wealth.

•••••

National Speakers Association Annual Conference, Southern California, summer of 1997.
About two thousand speakers in attendance from
all over the world. Pros at the podium. Masters at
their craft.

In his workshop at that NSA conference, Doug
Malouf, professional speaker and trainer from Aus-
tralia, offered the following amusing gem: ***Whenever
an adult (or adolescent) audience is sitting and
listening for longer than seven minutes at a
time, the minds in that audience begin to drift
into sexual fantasy – and no speaker or teacher
can compete with that!***

In another NSA session, it was noted: ***Lecture for
ninety minutes and learners will HEAR it; lecture for twenty minutes and learners will
UNDERSTAND it; involve learners every eight
minutes in the lecture and they will KNOW AND
REMEMBER it.***

Basically *Sharing the Wealth IS* the lecture piece,
the information-giving part. But there's more to this
step than simply telling your students what they
need to know. It's a giving and receiving of wealth,
i.e. information, in a reciprocal manner. It's an active step in the map, not a passive one.

***Sharing the Wealth is about your students con-
necting new information with old and using***

activities and conversation to explore those connections.

But you say you've got a lot of information and little time to deliver it? You've *GOT* to lecture to fit it all in. They *HAVE* to listen in order to "get it." Right? Not quite! A nugget from **Presenting with Pizzazz** bears repeating here:

> *If you want them to HEAR it, you talk.*
> *If you want them to LEARN it, they talk.*

Okay, okay, you protest! You got the point but you still have a problem with fitting it all in, especially when you have tons of content to cover in a specific amount of time. After all, giving your students free reign to chat about stuff can eat up a lot of valuable minutes.

Again, the solution is simple: you make the involvement a standard part of your lecture. Every ten minutes or so you stop your lecture and have your students do a quick activity or dialogue that engages them in the content. By using pairs, triads, small groups, writing, note-taking, fill-in-the-blanks, doodle drawings, pair-shares, personal reflections (all in the *Sharing the Wealth Flight Kit)* you can structure the activity so that it doesn't take much time (if time is an issue) but is nevertheless rich in learner-centered involvement. You can be the timekeeper and keep the interaction as short as 15 - 30 seconds if you wish. It's all up to you.

There is a secret and powerful by-product of this learner-centered lecture. Bob Pike, in his **Creative Training Techniques Handbook,** points out: **"One of my 'Laws of Adult Learning' is that 'people don't argue with their own data.' If I say some-**

thing, I've got to believe it; after all I'm teaching it. But if a participant says something, he or she will accept and believe it more fervently." And that applies to learners of all ages. Students tend to use new information more readily if they "own it" first. Talking about it is the first step to owning it.

Besides that, as teachers and trainers, we tire ourselves out when we do all the talking. Spencer Kagan, in his marvelous manual *Cooperative Learning,* reminds us:

> *It's no wonder that teachers*
> *in traditional classrooms*
> *end up so exhausted.*
> *They are bucking*
> *the basic nature of the student.*
> *Students want to question,*
> *discuss, argue, and share.*

So don't buck it! Go with the flow and make the questioning, discussing, arguing, and sharing an integral part of your *Step Two* presentation. **Give your learners information as well as time to share reactions, insights, frustrating questions, and flashes of understanding with each other and with you in multiple ways.** Yes, you *CAN* do your dynamite delivery of golden nuggets of knowledge. Just make sure your learners get their chance to shine also.

By the way, asking *"Are there any questions?"* doesn't cut it! How many times have you asked that question only to look out over a sea of faces and motionless bodies, waiting for a hand to go up – and one never does? Then you say, *"Okay, if there aren't any questions, we'll move on."* How many times have you sat in a class, heard that question, and thought, *"No way am I raising my hand here. I'll wait until a break to ask my question."* Asking, *"Are there any questions?"* is more often than not a sure way to silence a group. What to do instead? Say, *"You have 30 seconds to turn to a neighbor and tell that person one question you may still have about what you just learned."* Wait for 30 seconds and then say, *"Would one or two of you please share with the whole group the question your partner asked?"* A far more involving and thought-provoking experience for all.

Or give it a twist: Instead of having your students come up with questions, you write a question down for all to see about what you just presented and have them pair up and answer it. Or you write three words or phrases from your lesson and tell them these are the answers to three questions. Now they have 30 seconds to phrase the questions and tell a partner what they are.

A pet peeve of mine is when I hear a teacher or trainer announce, *"Now WE'RE going to discuss ..."* and then proceed to do all the talking while I and the rest of the class get to do all the listening. Come on! Involve me in the discussion too so that it's really a *WE* and not a *ME ONLY.* How? Again, ask me to dialogue for a few seconds with a person to my right (left, behind, in front). Then invite me to share my thought, idea, reaction with the whole group (or to share someone else's thought, idea, reaction). Doesn't take much time and I'm with you now every step of the way.

One final thought: Do *YOU* believe in your heart and soul that your learners' knowledge is as important as your own? That they should have a chance to share their reactions to your information? Or do you think that all this is irrelevant to the learning process? That they can talk about the information on their own time but right now you have a lot of stuff to cover so you want them to be quiet and listen? Bernice McCarthy warns us:

Technique is never value neutral.

If you choose lecture as your sole means of delivering information in *Step Two,* you are in effect saying to your learners that you value what *YOU* have to say more than what *THEY* have to say. *And at times that may be the message you want to deliver.* There may even be times when your students *WANT* you to do all the talking, especially if you embellish your lecture with entertaining vignettes, stories, and amusing anecdotes which help your students remember the information you're presenting to them. Or there may be other times when you have so much material to cover that you decide to go for *QUANTITY* rather than *QUALITY.* All you can do is hope your students learn as much as they can from the lectures and reading material (quite honestly, some will and some won't). By the way, the quantity vs. quality issue *NEVER* goes away. It's a balancing act which all teachers and trainers struggle with on a daily basis. Sometimes you can indeed combine both, but more often than not (especially due to time constraints), one is sacrificed a bit for the other.

Having said that, if you *DO* decide to make *Step Two* interactive so that your students are involved in the learning, your message to them is very different: **how they feel and what they think IS indeed an important part of the learning process.** In fact, real learning can't take place effectively without this student involvement.

Learning ...
a never-ending negotiation
between new information and
what (learners) already know.
...Elizabeth Christopher
and Larry Smith

What does it matter if we teach a person
to read and to write and to paragraph
if we lose the essence of that person?
...John Bradshaw

Knowledge needs to be a verb.
...Anonymous

How tired I feel!
I understood so much today.
...Ashleigh Brilliant

Ground School

•••••

1. Label the following "yes" or "no":

A. *Step Two is straight lecture.*

B. *Sharing the Wealth builds knowledge and understanding.*

C. *Step Two connects people to content through involvement in the learning.*

D. *One way of involving your students in Step Two is to have them talk about what they've learned and how it relates to what they already know.*

E. *Every 45 minutes of lecture should be followed by a Sharing the Wealth activity.*

F; *Learner involvement in Step Two can be as short or as long as you wish.*

G. *A good rule of thumb is to break up a lecture every ten minutes or so with a quick Sharing the Wealth activity.*

H. *It helps your students learn more effectively if they wait until the class is over to talk about what they're learning.*

I. *Students remember more of the lecture when they get a chance to question, argue, discuss, and react to the information presented in Step Two.*

And the answers: N Y Y Y N Y Y N Y. Good going!

2. Cross out the items that do *NOT* contain all the elements of a successful *Sharing The Wealth* piece:

A. *Mike lectures to his high school students for about forty minutes on the history of computers before he invites discussion.*

B. *During her lecture, Cindee directs her community college math students to draw pictorial representations of the math concept they're studying. Then they share the pictures with a partner.*

C. *Shawna asks her middle school science class rhetorical questions then answers her own questions as the students listen.*

D. *During his lecture, Oliver makes sure his training participants take notes and write down questions they want to discuss after the lecture.*

E. *About every ten minutes, Julie has her high school history class students turn to a neighbor and repeat one important thing they just learned from the lecture.*

F. *Alex has so much information to give his adult trainees that he saves the question and answer period until the end of the day.*

Did you cross out A C F? Fantabulous!

3. **Write your own definition of *Sharing The Wealth* in the left margin of this page.**

4. **What is one way you can make your lectures more interactive? (Take a look at the *Sharing The Wealth Flight Kit*.)**

5. **Ask a teacher or trainer friend what he does to involve his students in the learning. Write his answer in the right margin.**

Chapter Eight: Making It Happen.

Chapter Eight:
Making It Happen.
• • • • •

I once attended a communication skills seminar where we sat all day and listened to the presenter talk about how to talk. She told us the steps to take when we wanted to solve a communication problem, and how to really listen, and what to say when we didn't understand something. *She lectured to us about communicating but we never had the chance to walk the talk.* Did the seminar change the ways I communicated? Nope. Did I remember what she said? Not much. Was I willing to try some of the communication techniques she listed? Not on your life. I had no idea how they would feel or if they would work in real life.

What was lacking in the seminar? Hands-on experience. Good old Albert Einstein put it this way:

Learning IS experience.
Everything else is just information.

It's a complete waste of time to learn about a skill without practicing it. It's a little like watching a video which teaches you how to ski. When the video is over, do you know how to ski? Probably not. If you want to learn how to ski, you go skiing. If you want to learn how to communicate, you practice talking and listening. If you're learning about problem-solving, you have to solve some problems. **You need to do something with the information you've heard in order to really learn it, to make it your own. And so do your students.**

Step Three is about practice, skill-building, and using what has been learned. In *Step One,* you helped your students connect with each other and with the topic of the class or training. In *Step Two* you gave them important information and allowed them some time to react, to question, to discuss. ***Now they need to begin using the information in practical and useful ways.*** So you give your students time to tinker with the new material and to create ways to adapt it to their respective lives.

> **Simply put, new information**
> **does not become their own**
> **until they do something with it.**

Since *Step Three* is about *DOING,* the learning environment will look busy, sound noisy, and will have a feeling of concentration, energy, and intensity as students work alone and together to create new ways of doing things with what they've just learned. As Bob Pike describes, your learners will be ***"developing their own answers, applying tools and techniques, using reference manuals, and tapping their own resources and those of their colleagues to reach solutions that work, both in class and on the job."***

I'm not telling you anything new here. You already know the value of experience. You might want to check in with your own beliefs, though, to see how you *REALLY* feel about becoming the "guide-on-the-side" at this point. Do you really believe that an experience is a more powerful way of learning than listening? Do you believe your students will remember *WHAT THEY DO* more than *WHAT YOU SAY?* Do you believe they need some practice time in your class or training? Or do you think they can do their own practice on their own time after the class is over? *If you're convinced by now (or have been convinced for a long time) that experience is needed for any learning to be successful, then you'll automatically want to follow the information-sharing step with the practice and skill-building step.*

During this step, your students might become involved in projects in which they use the information learned. *Or this step might actually include real life skills practiced in or out of the classroom.* Note that I said "in or out" – practicing a skill can take place a number of different ways in a number of different places. Students can create simulations of real life events to be presented in the classroom, or they can actually practice the event in real life (example: a community college class simulation of a job interview or experiencing a mock interview with an employer-friend). Students can go out into the community gathering information to complete a special project. Or they can go into other classes to practice their skills within the school (I know a high school speech teacher who had her students find students from other classes who would act as listeners while the speech class students rehearsed their speeches). On the adult level, if the class or training is ongoing, students can practice their skills with family members, friends, or colleagues. Can the *Making It Happen* step be assigned as homework? Of course. Should the results of the homework be brought back to the class to be discussed and evaluated? Absolutely.

Making It Happen doesn't need to take hours and hours. *Like the other steps, this one can be as short or as long as you wish.* And if you're teaching more than one skill, you may want to skip back and forth between *Step Two* and *Step Three:* a little information, a little skill practice, more information, more skill-building. and so on. Elementary teachers do this naturally since younger children learn best by combining a bit of information with a bit of hands-on practice. Guess what? Older children – and adults – learn the same ways as kids and need to practice with the content just like younger ones do. It was a major informational mistake of the past decade to think that kids and adults learn in different ways (remember the "androgogy vs. pedagogy" nonsense?). The four learning styles apply to all learners regardless of their ages. *All four learning styles need to experience the Making It Happen step of the styles map.*

Use the *Making It Happen Flight Kit* to create your own flight plan with the map, one that will work for you and your students.

Natural knowledge
is knowledge that can be applied
in real-world situations.
...Renate Cain

Thought, creativity and learning
arise from experience.
...Carla Hannaford

My great ambition
is to build something that will last,
at least until I've finished building it.
...Ashleigh Brilliant

Ground School

• • • • •

1. *Making It Happen* can include: (check all that apply):

A. *students working on projects in which they use the information they've learned.*

B. *students practicing skills outside the classroom.*

C. *students reading a textbook or coursebook for homework and doing nothing else with the information read.*

D. *students creating simulations and role-plays in which they practice their skills in the classroom.*

E. *students taking tests about what they've learned.*

F. *students working with other students.*

G. *students seeking out your help when they need it as they practice their skills.*

H. *students listening to a lecture about the subject.*

Did you check A B D F G? Far out!

How about E? Well, you can include an assessment activity like a test in any step of the map. In *Step Three*, your students still need time to build skills and practice using the material learned even if they take a test.

2. Circle the items that describe *Step Three:*

A. *Howard divides his middle school video technology class into small work groups where the students develop video projects to present to the school later in the year.*

B. Carolyn has her adult trainees pair up to practice communication skills.

C. Richard instructs his high school math students
on the correct way to solve an algebraic equation.

D. Bev reads a story about mammals to her elementary science class to illustrate what they are
studying.

E. Barbara makes sure her community college resume writing class spends enough time writing
mock resumes before the students put together
their final ones.

Awesome if you circled A B E!

3. Write your definition of *Step Three*.

**4. Jot down two *Making It Happen* activities
you've done in your classes or trainings before reading this book.**

**5. Now add one more activity to that list – an
activity you're promising yourself to try in
your next class or training. (Need an idea?
Take a look at the *Making It Happen Flight
Kit*.)**

Chapter Nine:
Celebrating Success.

Chapter Nine:
Celebrating Success.

• • • • •

Think back to one of the happiest days of your life. What was the occasion? What was happening? Where were you? Who was there with you? I'll bet you that, whatever the occasion, it most probably had to do with some kind of celebration. A graduation, perhaps. Or the birth of your child. A marriage. A special vacation. A team win. A holiday. A spiritual transformation. A goal achieved. And you probably remember most of the details about the day: the people, sights, sounds, smells, colors, feelings. All of it. Ah, wonderful memories!

Celebrations make an experience memorable, and a classroom or training room experience is no exception. A celebration shines a spotlight on an event as if to say, *"Pay attention. This is a special moment. Never to be forgotten."*

That's why celebrations are so important: they help us remember things long after the celebrating is over.

Step Four is about celebrating and remembering, coming full circle, wrapping it up, bringing it home. David Kolb in **Experiential Learning** has a lovely phrase for describing this step: **the "transformation dimension" where the learner identifies his changes in thought and action that have occurred as a result of the learning experience.**

Actually, *Celebrating Success* is a jumping-off place, a place where your students pull together everything they've learned and decide what to do with it once they leave the classroom or training room.

And how do your students feel as they experience this piece? Excited about trying out the new stuff they've learned. Anxious to explore its uses in their own lives. Eager to learn more. Willing to make a commitment to do just that. What a wonderful way to leave a learning experience! *High on the learning and on the possibilities of new things to do with it.*

Step Four is really three-pieces-in-one:

1. Students celebrate themselves and the learning journey they've taken together;

2. Students share their new knowledge with each other in a variety of ways;

3. Students make a commitment (an action plan) to use the new information in their own lives once they leave the learning environment.

Bob Pike in **The Best of the Creative Training Techniques Newsletter** gives teachers and trainers three questions to think about so they can make sure all the pieces in *Step Four* are present:

1. Does it allow celebration, i.e., does it reinforce what participants have achieved, what they have accomplished?

2. Does it reinforce the learning? Does it somehow summarize what people have gained so they realize they are taking something back with them?

3. Does it provide impetus for back-on-the-job application (or, in the case of classroom instruction, real-life application outside of the learning environment)?

If the truth be told, *Celebrating Success* is another connection piece, with an eye on the future this time. Your students connect with each other once again as well as with the important information they've learned. *But the emphasis is on what they plan to do with what they've learned, and how they feel about it all.*

Without some kind of closure to the learning experience, students kind of scatter to the four winds with no real focus on where they've been or where they're going. *Step Four* helps them take stock of their learning and decide what to do with it when they leave. In addition, *Celebrating Success* creates positive feelings about learning so students will want to continue learning even after they leave.

By the way, *Celebrating Success* doesn't necessarily have to happen in the classroom or training room. Susan Kovalik, author of **Teachers Make The Difference,** insists that community action be a part of *Step Four.* She explains that students should take what they've learned out into the community in some way: letters to the editor, community projects, public service, political involvement.

Some examples of Celebrating Success: In an elementary school setting, *Step Four* could include students presenting displays, programs, or projects for other classes, Parents' Night, Open House, etc. At the high school level, *Celebrating Success* could be a community performance, a presentation to a local organization, a school-wide program, or a write-up in the local newspaper. In community college human resource development programs where people learn job skills, *Step Four* may include learners experiencing actual job interviews or being hired for real jobs. In all cases, there needs to be an acknowledgment of the learning gained and the connections made. Step Four brings the learning full circle.

The celebration part of *Step Four* can also include activities where students acknowledge the helpfulness of their classmates, their own growth, and the best parts of the learning experience. The *Celebrating Success Flight Kit* gives you a number of ideas to think about and try. Change them to fit your own goals.

Again, the important question is: How do *YOU* feel about celebrations? Unnecessary to learning? Frivolous? A waste of time? Essential to remembering? A great way to wrap up a lesson or training? A way to get learners to want more? Your beliefs about the importance of this step will influence how you organize it and how much time you put into it.

As with the other steps, this one does not need to be lengthy if time is short. ***The point is to get your students to focus one more time on what they've learned and what they plan to do with it.***

> ***Break the mold ...***
> ***Make it fun ...***
> ***Change the pace ...***
> ***ANYTHING can be made special.***
> ...Tom Peters

When your soul is happy
your learning is snappy.

...David Meier

If you don't do it, you'll never know
what would have happened
if you had done it.

...Ashleigh Brilliant

Ground School

·····

1. Put a star beside the items which describe a necessary element of *Step Four:*

A. You give your students last-minute information about the subject.

B. You make sure your students have time to say what they appreciated about working together.

C. Your students create ways to use the information in their own lives outside the classroom.

D. Your students do further research on the subject.

E. Your students pass a test.

F. Students receive awards.

G. Students share with each other what they valued about the learning experience and how they plan to use what they've learned.

H. Students leave feeling good about what they've learned.

Did you star B C G H? You're flying high!

Items A D E F can also be a part of *Step Four* if you wish. They aren't *NECESSARY* though.

2. Which letter *BEST* describes a *Step Four* activity?

A. Kathy always includes an upbeat energizer in her closing activities so that everyone leaves her adult training feeling good about the day.

B. *Paul arranges for his high school Spanish students to enjoy a dinner together at a local Hispanic restaurant.*

C. *Edwina has her welfare to-work trainees share their successful job-seeking experiences, participate in an awards luncheon, and plan what they're going to do next.*

D. *Joseph allows time for his elementary students to tell the class the most important things they learned from the history unit.*

Did you choose C? Way cool!

3. Which letter does *NOT* describe any part of *Step Four*?

A. *Linda's middle school physical education classes play a final round of softball games using all the skills taught during the semester.*

B. *Tim's adult training on peer-coaching skills ends with coaches practicing the skills in real-life situations then reporting back to him their evaluations of the real-life coaching experience.*

C. *Ray's community college computer class students demonstrate their familiarity with a certain software program by teaching the basics to another computer class.*

D. *Once Matty's high school geography class has memorized the locations of the Seven Wonders of the World, they go on to study the topographical characteristics of the various countries.*

Of course you chose D!

4. **In the box, draw a doodle representing your understanding of *Celebrating Success*.**

5. **What is one closing activity that you do which meets some or all of the *Step Four* elements?**

6. **What is another *Celebrating Success* activity you might be willing to try? (Refer to the *Celebrating Success Flight Kit*.)**

Chapter Ten:
Bringing It Home.

Chapter Ten:
Bringing It Home.

·····

You're a student pilot on that last long-distance solo cross-country flight. You have to fly the triangle-shaped course you charted on your flight map, landing at two other airports before heading home. It's part of the game-plan, hitting the designated stops along the way.

Let's change the metaphor for a moment. Instead of flying, think baseball. Four bases. Gotta touch them all if you want a home-run. And usually you have to touch them in order – it would make for a funny ballgame if you didn't!

The same goes for the styles map. Think of it as a teaching and learning flight plan to help you move your students from where they are to where you want them to go. **Four stops. Four bases. Four steps. And all four need to be in a lesson or training so that you can all arrive "home."** You can't get there without including all the steps along the way. Oh, sure, in all reality, you *CAN* teach a lesson without using the map, or by using some but not all of the steps. The learning just won't *WORK* as well for your students, that's all. Some of them will get it and some of them won't. No big deal, unless you want to make sure that most of them get it most of the time. If that's the case, the map is your guide to making it happen.

So you've got a lesson to teach or a training to give. **You know there will be four main pieces to your** *lesson or training: Getting Connected (Preparation), Sharing The Wealth (Presentation), Making It Happen (Practice), and Celebrating Success (Performance).* You need to be clear about what it is you're planning to teach. You need to choose activities which will involve your students in their own learning during each of the four pieces or steps of the lesson. All the activities you choose will connect your students to the information you're giving them. Many of the activities will connect your students to each other as well. And you have to keep within the time limit of the class or training. If you have an ongoing class, you may decide to do the connecting piece one day, the information piece another, and so on. If you have a onetime training session, you'll do all four steps in the time allotted.

You have some questions to ask yourself now:

- *What is the subject or topic I plan to teach? Can it be done in one lesson or do I need to plan a number of lessons to cover it all?*

- *What do I want my students to be able to do after they learn the information?*

- *How do I plan to connect my students to each other and to the topic in Step One?*

- *How do I plan to present the information while at the same time involving them in the learning in Step Two?*

- *What kind of practice activities would be the most useful for them in Step Three?*

- **What do I want them to make a commitment to do after the class is over? How do I want them to celebrate the learning in Step Four?**

- **How will I be able to tell if they've learned it or not?**

- **How much time do I need in order to cover all of the steps? How much time should I spend on each step? Each activity?**

The map is your flight plan but you determine how long you're going to linger at each step. You may even decide you want to mix up the pieces a bit. Certainly, your students will need to make connections at the beginning of the lesson and enjoy a celebration at the end. But you may decide to flip-flop the two middle steps, moving back and forth between them as you give your students some information and have them do something with it. Then a bit more knowledge and a bit more practice. And so on.

You may want to spend a longer period of time in *Steps Two* and *Three* so you shorten up *Steps One* and *Four.* You may have two activities for *Step One* and four activities for *Step Three.* Or you may keep it simple and have only one activity for each piece. You may spend a long while in *Step One* connecting your students to the subject, then in *Step Two* have them work independently as they gather the information on their own. Or you may have the first three steps end with a grand performance in *Step Four* where a lot of time is spent having students present to other classes what they've learned. Remember, not all steps need to be done in your classroom or training room. Students can work on pieces at home, at school, or in the larger community. ***The bottom line is: it's all up to you! You design it the way you think it'll work best for your learners. You give it your total attention and your personal best, then you allow the learning to happen.***

Alley oops! What if it doesn't work the way you planned it? What if you make some mistakes? No problem! *Among pilots, a successful landing is any landing that you can walk away from.* Here's another comforting pilot-type thought: ***ANYTHING'S better than crashing!*** Kind of puts things in perspective when your classroom's in chaos (which *WILL* happen on occasion, map or no map!). Can you walk away after it's all over? Isn't it still better than crashing? And can you figure out which pieces worked, which didn't, why, and what to do about it for the next time? Then it's a successful landing, my friend, and you need to cut yourself some slack as you fine-tune your lesson and tinker again with the steps of the styles map.

Let me show you how I use the map to plan one of my own trainings:* I'm going to be teaching effective communication skills to a group of adults. The training will last about five hours. I want the training participants to leave knowing their own communication strengths and weaknesses, how to listen to others, and how to communicate in ways which may not be comfortable for them. ***I'm clear about what I want to teach and what I want them to leave knowing how to do.***

So I draw a simple map with four steps on it (which is nothing more than taking a blank piece of paper and dividing it into four sections with the step numbers and labels). I begin the work of filling in the map. I take out my *Flight Kit* (in this case I use the

Getting Connected activities in this book) and choose one or two activities which will be good connecting ones for this particular training. I choose *Take A Stand* and *Four Corners* because I can list communication style characteristics a number of different times so that the training participants are moving, dialoguing, and connecting to their own communication strengths and weaknesses while they get to know each other. That's *Step One.*

In *Step Two* I have participants take a *Pop Quiz* about communication styles, do *Doodle Drawings* representing their own strengths and weaknesses, take notes during the lecture, and do a couple of quick *Pair Shares* to review what they've learned (all these activities are in the *Sharing The Wealth Flight Kit*).

In *Step Three,* they practice active listening and style-stretching with a partner. Then I have them do *Each One Teach One* (in the *Making It Happen Flight Kit*) to review the skills they've practiced.

Finally, in *Step Four,* small groups create *Victorious Vignettes* – role-plays in which they act out real life communication situations using the two skills they've learned: active listening and style-stretching. Groups applaud each other. A quick *Koosh Throw* ends the training where they share how they plan to use these skills in their own lives (activities from the *Celebrating Success Flight Kit*). They give each other compliments as part of the celebration too. My metaphorical gift to them as they walk out the door are pairs of soft plastic ears to wear to remind them that one of the most effective communication skills is listening.

I filled in the pieces of my training map with activities that fit my goals, the objectives of

***each step, and my training participants' learn-
ing needs.*** All the activities centered around effective communication. All the activities connected the
participants to the topic as well as to each other.
All the activities fit within the time limit under which
I was working. I presented the styles map steps in
order because it worked better for my learners that
way. ***Because all four steps were present, the
learning style preferences of my training participants were honored and each person got a
chance to learn in a way that was best for him.***

That's it in a nutshell. The map can be as simple or
as complicated a teaching tool as you wish to make
it. Hopefully, after reading this book, it feels simple
enough to you so that you'll feel eager to use it, to
play with it, to see how it works for you and your
students. As you get more proficient in applying it
to your own teaching, you may want to take a class
or training to learn more about the many ways you
can adapt and refine it to create even more successful learning experiences.

A home-based example: Many years ago, when my
husband and I were teaching our foster son Dominic
(a ten-year old handicapped child) a morning routine to follow on school days, we used the map without even knowing it. *Step One* was the buy-in part.
We showed Dominic our own morning routine and
how much time it saved us. Dominic wanted to
watch morning cartoons before school so he could
see the benefit of using the time he saved to get to
do that. *Step Two* was the informational part. We
helped Dominic make a chart with all the morning
routine chores: make bed, brush teeth, comb hair,
get dressed, etc. We discussed and listed all the
essentials and indicated criteria that needed to be
met (one swatch of the comb with Dominic's cow-

licks still all akimbo was not an acceptable hair-combing method). When the chart was finished, Dominic used it as a daily plan and starred each completed item – that was *Step Three.* His immediate *Step Four* celebration was to check in with us for his morning "inspection" which he loved because of the praise and attention he received for a job well done, then fifteen minutes of cartoon viewing time. The long term *Celebrating Success* was a family outing at the end of the week, an allowance, and later on, making the morning chores a little more challenging as he became more proficient (making his own breakfast, for example). **It was the map in action and it worked. You may not have realized it until now, but you too use it all the time – now you just know how it works and why!**

In piloting an airplane, you have to learn how to first keep the plane level while flying before you can practice turns, banks, slips and stalls, Level flight is the beginner's goal.

**Using the styles map
as described in this book
is your experience
with level flight.**

To help you make your own flight plans using the map, I've included some blank flight plan pages in this chapter. Remember, you also have four *Flight Kits* at your fingertips. Furthermore, if you want to see how other teachers and trainers use the styles map, **The Center for Accelerated Learning** offers an incredible collection of lessons and activities in their **Accelerated Learning Course Builder** (another "flight kit" you won't want to be without. See the *Resources* section in this book). So climb into that pilot's seat and go for it!

First, have a definite,
clear, practical ideal –
a goal, an objective.
Second, have the necessary means
to achieve your ends –
wisdom, money,
materials and methods.
Third, adjust all your means
to that end.

...Aristotle

The cycle is the key.
It is the cycle that brings balance
and wholeness to learning...
Clearly, the dance itself is the thing.

...Bernice McCarthy

If you want to put yourself
on the map,
publish your own map.

...Ashleigh Brilliant

My Flight Plan For:

Title/Content:

Duration:

Step One: Getting Connected

Step Two: Sharing The Wealth

Step Three: Making It Happen

Step Four: Celebrating Success

My Flight Plan For:

Title/Content:

Duration:

Step One: Getting Connected

Step Two: Sharing The Wealth

Step Three: Making It Happen

Step Four: Celebrating Success

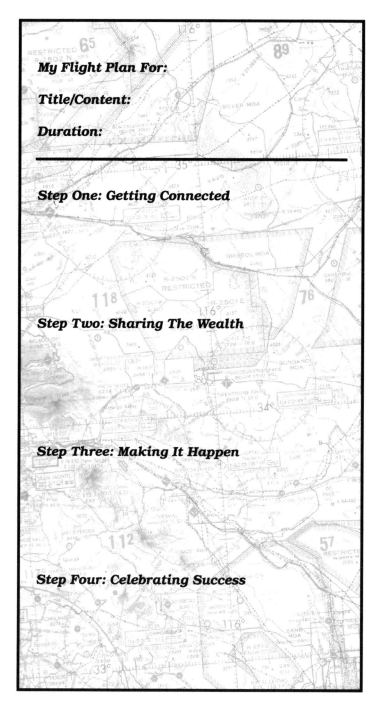

My Flight Plan For:

Title/Content:

Duration:

Step One: Getting Connected

Step Two: Sharing The Wealth

Step Three: Making It Happen

Step Four: Celebrating Success

My Flight Plan For:

Title/Content:

Duration:

Step One: Getting Connected

Step Two: Sharing The Wealth

Step Three: Making It Happen

Step Four: Celebrating Success

Chapter Eleven:
The Joy Is In The Journey.

Chapter Eleven:
The Joy Is In The Journey.
• • • • •

*T*HE DAY has finally arrived. One of the scariest and most challenging days of your life. One year of ground school and flight lessons leading up to this day. Three long distance solo cross-country flights behind you. Four weeks of daily flying practice in all kinds of weather. Drills in slow flight, stalls, soft-field and short field landings, go arounds, steep banks and turns, slips, emergency landings, instrument failures, night flying, and on and on until you can hear the Cessna's noisy drone in your sleep.

The day of your FAA flight exam. Windy. Storm clouds building over the mountains. Definitely not the most ideal conditions. The FAA instructor Rick, a quiet soft-spoken man, figures you'll finish the flying portion of the test before the storm hits the airport – small comfort to you as you watch the gusts whirl the windsock in all directions. **You take a deep breath and once again remind yourself that you'll be giving each moment your total attention and your personal best.** It doesn't mean flying like the pros do. It doesn't mean perfection – you know you're probably going to make some mistakes (hopefully minor ones). You're simply going to use everything you've learned up to this point to make this your best flying day ever. And if you pass the test, more power to you!

And you *DO* pass – with *FLYING* colors (excuse the pun!). You're as high as the clouds closing in! And

Rick is right – the storm hits the airport just as you touch down. Talk about timing! As Rick shakes your hand and gives you the slip of paper that is your pilot's license, he asks, *"Do you know what this means? It means you now have official permission to learn how to fly."* What an odd thing to say: *permission to learn how to fly.* But you've already learned how to fly. On second thought, maybe you haven't. Maybe you've just started learning to fly and the flight exam is one small step in the journey.

After Rick congratulates you, he continues, *"How do you plan to use your pilot's license? Business? Recreation? Where do you plan to go? What's your next step? Instrument-rating? Bigger planes? How about retractable gear? High performance? Multi-engine? Ever thought about commercial flying?"* Yup. This test is a big step for you but a small step when you look at the whole picture. Whoa! You could spend your whole life flying and, at the end of it, still have more to learn.

Lots of people have written and spoken the words that are rattling around inside your head at this point: **Life isn't a destination. It's a journey.** Flying is simply a metaphor for life. And for learning.

Then another revelation hits you like a bolt from the blue: **Like flying, the styles map is a metaphor for life itself. The four steps actually represent four aspects of living.** Wait a minute. Where did that thought come from? Other thoughts crowd in on the heels of the first: *Getting Connected* is about emotional relationships. *Sharing The Wealth* is about mental creativity. *Making It Happen* is about physical productivity. And *Celebrating Success* is about spiritual growth. **Emotional, mental, physi-**

cal, spiritual. Four facets of life. Four sides of yourself. Four roads on a map.

A final burst of brilliant thinking: The map can be used as a guide to balance these aspects of yourself on a daily basis. You realize you can map out your day so that each of the four facets is experienced in some way. And when one aspect is missing and your day feels a little out-of-balance, you can use the map to figure out which piece isn't there and pull it back in somehow so that balance is restored.

How does that work? Let's say you're feeling a little down emotionally. You look at the map and realize that you haven't done anything physical all day long. So you take a long walk and find your emotional state shifting to more positive feelings.

Or maybe you've spent the entire day doing mental kinds of things: reports, paperwork, agendas, projects, and the like. You feel uptight and harried. You check out the map and notice that you haven't given yourself any spiritual time – to pray, reflect, meditate, create, or just play. You take a break and begin to do something that gives you a lot of joy. Or you pick up the Bible or another inspirational book. Or you just sit quietly for a few minutes and think about all the things you're grateful for.

Perhaps your day has been a whirlwind of doing, doing, doing. You think about the map and know that what you need most is a quiet hour with your spouse, significant other, or best friend to help you feel connected again.

It's about balance. It's about life. It's about learning. And it never ends.

The joy is in the journey.

So, my friend, take joy in your journey! And since this book has been a part of your travels, I encourage you to spend a moment right now patting yourself on the back for completing this piece. Better yet, go outside and let loose a coyote whoop! Dance a little jig in your driveway. Invite a friend over for ice-cream. Tell a loved one about what you've learned so far and how you plan to use it the next time you have to teach something to someone. ***Celebrate your own success! You know a whole lot more now about how to give it so they get it. And now you can indeed, teach anyone anything and make it stick!***

> *Joy is the feeling*
> *of grinning inside.*
> *...Melba Colgrove*

> *"On with the dance,*
> *let the joy be unconfined!"*
> *is my motto;*
> *whether there's any dance to dance*
> *or any joy to unconfine.*
> *...Mark Twain*

> *Where will it all end?*
> *Probably somewhere near*
> *where it all began.*
> *...Ashley Brilliant*

*T*here *are journeys*
upon journeys,
Journeys inward and
journeys outward;
Some spiraling us down
into ourselves,
And some flinging us up
into the night sky
amidst the shooting stars.

...Sharon Bowman

Flight Kits

How to Give It So They Get It

Flight Kits

· · · · ·

*Your own
beginning collection
of activities and ideas
geared to each
of the four steps
of the styles map.*

Getting Connected Flight Kit

• • • • •

All of these activities connect people to people and people to content. Remember, even if your students already know each other well, the connecting activities still help to connect your students in personal and meaningful ways to the topic of your lesson or training. And these activities help keep the learning community alive and the trust level and feelings of safety strong. You can always change the introductory questions to ones that review previous lessons you've already taught about the subject. *A reminder: Take what you can use and let go of the rest.*

Notes:

Getting Connected Activity #1:
Take-A-Stand

A wonderfully versatile little activity that can be used a number of different ways with both large and small groups of students.

General Instructions: You tell the students there is an imaginary line down the center of the room with one end of the line standing for something related to the topic (an issue, a statement, a question) and the other end standing for the opposite. Students take-a-stand at either one end or the other or any place in between. Then they introduce themselves to those standing nearest them and explain why they chose to stand where they did. You can repeat the activity a few times with different issues, statements, or questions. After each repetition, you ask discussion questions similar to the following:

• *Why did you decide to stand where you're standing?*

• *What did you notice about the group?*

• *What did you learn about yourself?*

Set-Up/Materials: Nothing special is needed. The activity takes about 5 - 15 minutes depending upon how many repetitions you include.

Examples: At a communication skills training, one end of the line stood for *"think before you speak"* and the other end stood for *"speak before you think."* In a job development workshop, one end stood for *"have held the same job for a long time"* and the other stood for *"have changed jobs a lot in my career."* In a college technology class one end was *"hates computers"* and the other end was *"loves computers."* In an elementary school science class, one end stood for *"yes,"* the other end *"no,"* and the teacher asked questions related to the science unit being studied. You can have one end represent *"strongly agree"* and the other end represent *"strongly disagree."* You can use humor, cliches, one-liners, catchy phrases to represent each end as long as they relate to the topic.

Notes:

Getting Connected Activity #2:
Four Corners

Another great activity that can be easily adapted to a variety of subject areas. Works better with larger groups (a dozen or more people).

General Instructions: Similar to *Take-A-Stand*, you designate each of the four corners of the room to represent something related to the topic. Learners go to one of the four corners (or between corners, or the middle of the room if undecided) and dialogue with those standing near them why they chose that corner. Then you ask for a few volunteers to share their answers with the whole group. You can also change the descriptions of the corners and have them do the activity again.

Set-Up/Materials: No extra set-up or materials are required unless you want to visually label each corner with the phrase representing it. Time needed is 5 - 15 minutes depending upon how many repetitions you do.

Examples: In a college stress management course, each of the four corners represented four major stressors: *"job, health, time, money."* At a teacher training, the four corners represented *"strongly agree, moderately agree, moderately disagree, strongly disagree,"* and issues related to education were stated with teachers moving to the corner that most accurately represented how they felt about each issue. In a parenting styles workshop, the four corners were labeled animals' names as metaphors representing the four parenting styles: *"golden retriever, beaver, lion, otter."* You can get really creative and have the corners stand for shapes, sounds, colors, songs, etc. that stand for aspects of the topic.

Notes:

Getting Connected Activity #3:
Gallery Walk

From my book ***Presenting with Pizzazz***, this activity is equally effective in other steps of the styles map as well. It's a marvelous way to gather a lot of topic-related information while at the same time connecting people to people. And the information collected during the activity can be the jumping-off place for in-depth work later.

General Instructions: A number of large sheets of chart paper are taped to the walls of the room and spaced around the room so that students have to walk from one chart paper to the other. Each chart paper is labeled with a question, statement, or issue related to the topic. While upbeat music plays (optional), students walk around the room writing their responses on the charts. You can assign a direction to move or they can move randomly. They can do the activity as individuals or as small groups. After they've written on all the charts, they take a "gallery walk" or tour of the room, reading the charts and taking some notes on what they observe as they read. Finally, you discuss the activity with the whole group, having them share their observations, insights, etc. Examples of discussion questions are:

- *What interesting things did you notice as you read the charts?*
- *What written items were listed on more than one chart?*
- *What was something that you expected or didn't expect?*
- *What were some apparent patterns?*
- *What is a question you still have?*

Some general headings you may want to use on a few of the charts regardless of the topic are:

- *Your wishes for this class/training.*
- *Something you want to learn more about.*
- *Your strength (related to the topic).*
- *Your weakness (related to the topic).*

- *A question you want answered.*
- *One fact you know about the topic.*
- *How you feel about the topic.*

This activity can be an incredibly rich one depending upon how you phrase the chart headings and the type of information you want your learners to share.

Set-Up/Materials: You'll need to prepare the chart pages and tape them to the walls around the room before the activity begins. Enough walking space is needed so that students can move from chart to chart with ease. Each student will need a broad-tipped felt pen for chart writing, a note-taking page and regular pen or pencil. The activity will take from 10 - 30 minutes depending upon the size of the group, the number of chart pages (I usually have one chart page for every 3 - 5 learners), and the length of the class discussion.

Examples: In a high school human anatomy class, the charts were labeled with the various systems of the human body that were to be studied. At a change management training for a large company, the charts included: *"organizational changes that affect you; how you handle the changes; how others handle the changes; how you would like the company to handle the changes."* At a community college instructor's class, eight charts represented eight steps in a lesson design model and the activity was used as a review of information learned in a previous class.

Notes:

Getting Connected Activity #4:
People Scatter

An interesting variation on *Take A Stand* in which students can observe the diversity of their group as they spread out around the room.

General Instructions: You direct the whole group to stand in a line down the middle of the room (no particular order). You read two statements pertaining to the topic. If the first statement describes them, students take one step to the right of the line. If the second statement describes them they take one step to the left. You proceed to read a number of paired statements and students continue taking a step to the right or left depending upon which statement describes them the best. After six to eight statements, the group will be scattered all over the room. You ask them to tell the person or people they're standing closest to what the significance of the scatter is and then discuss the activity with the whole group. Your questions to the group can be:

* *What pattern is becoming evident?*
* *What is the significance of this pattern?*
* *What does the activity show us about the group?*
* *What does the activity show you about yourself?*

Set-Up/Materials: You need lots of space for this activity so that students can scatter without bumping into furniture. A breakout area at the back of the room works well. Or you can use another room, hallway, or go outside if weather permits. No other materials are necessary. The activity can accommodate small and large groups and will take about 5 - 15 minutes.

Examples: In an elementary class introducing the topic "community," the paired statements referred to the students' own communities: *big families, little families; few neighbors, lots of neighbors; a grocery store close enough to walk to, a grocery store you have to drive to.* At a leadership styles training, the paired statements described leadership qualities: *direct, indirect; action-oriented, people-oriented; doer, delegator; encourager, bottom-liner.* At a teacher's conference on human learning, the paired statements pertained to learning preferences: *feeling, thinking; active, reflective; whole to part, part to whole.* Again, you can get creative and use metaphors (sounds, colors, shapes, animals, kitchen objects, etc.), to represent qualities *("In managing stress, step to the right if you're more like a blender and to the left if you're more like a toaster." "In accounting, step to the left if you're more like the turtle and to the right if you're more like the hare").*

Notes:

Getting Connected Activity #5:
Mingle-Mingle

From **Presenting with Pizzazz,** a great energizer as well as connecting activity – kind of silly but fun at the same time.

General Instructions: At your signal, everyone in the room stands up and moves randomly around the room mumbling out loud, *"Mingle, mingle."* You give them 3 - 5 seconds to get sufficiently mixed up and then you sound a noisemaker (toy horn, whistle, hand claps). They stop moving, then turn to the person or people they're standing closest to, introduce themselves, and answer a question you've posted on a chart or overhead transparency. You give them a minute or two to dialogue, then repeat the activity using a different question next time. I usually repeat the activity three or four times so that learners have a chance to meet at least three or four other people and answer that many questions. Examples of questions to answer include:

- *Why did you decide to take this class/training?*
- *What are three things you know about the topic?*
- *What is one experience you've had that related to this topic?*
- *What do you want to know how to do when the class/ training is over?*

Set-Up/Materials: You write the questions on charts or overhead transparencies beforehand. Aisle space is needed so that people can move randomly around. Large groups (twenty or more people) work better for this activity. I've even seen it done successfully with 200 people! Time can be as short as 3 minutes or as long as 5 - 10 minutes depending upon the length of each dialogue time between "mingles."

Examples: At a speakers' workshop, participants mumbled *"Network, network,"* as they walked around the room, and the questions pertained to the topic: *"What was the most inspirational speech you've ever heard?*

*What are three things that make a speech work for you?
What is the one thing you would like to know how to do
better as a speaker?"* In a middle school math class the
words were: "*add, subtract, multiply, divide,*" and the
questions were math problems for which students had
to choose the appropriate function. For a stress management training, I changed the words the participants
said as they moved around the room to *"Relax, relax!"*
The questions then became: *"What really pushes your
buttons at work? What do you do about it when your
buttons get pushed? What do you want to learn from
this training?"*

Notes:

Getting Connected Activity #6:
People Hunt

There are as many variations to this activity as there are learners in your class or training. This is one of the easier ways of doing a *People Hunt*, a way that requires very little preparation time on your part.

General Instructions: Give each student a blank piece of 8 1/2 x 11 paper and a pen/pencil. Instruct them to fold the paper into 8 squares. They unfold the papers and fill in each square with their responses to the items you have listed on a chart or overhead transparency:

1. *Your wish for this class or training.*

2. *Your strength related to this topic.*

3. *Your weakness related to this topic.*

4. *A famous person who knows this topic well.*

5. *A doodle representing this topic.*

6. *A question you have about this topic.*

7. *A sound representing your feelings about this topic.*

8. *A one-liner describing this topic.*

You can also throw in one or two items that aren't topic related but are people-related: *"Your favorite movie. Your favorite junk food. Your favorite vacation spot."* After filling in their *People Hunt* papers, students circulate around the room (to upbeat music) and compare their answers. When they find a person who has a similar answer in any one of the boxes, that person writes his name in their box. The goal is to find as many people as possible who have similar answers and to gather as many different signatures as they can in the time allowed.

Set-Up/Materials: Prepare the listed items on a chart or overhead beforehand. Provide enough blank paper and writing tools for all participants. Allow 10 - 20 minutes for the activity depending upon the size of the group and the amount of time it takes for them to make their *People Hunt* papers.

Examples: One variation which many teachers and train-ers use is to create *People Hunt* handouts before the class or training. On the handouts are a list of sentences per-taining to the topic. Participants have to get signatures from people who match those sentences. In a college budgeting class, the sentences included: *"I balance my checkbook every month; I haven't a clue where my money goes; I know exactly how much I spend on clothes; When I want something I buy it; I spend every penny I earn; I save a little every month for a rainy day."* In a high school home economics class, the list included: *"I know the dif-ference between a tsp. and a tbsp; I've baked something from scratch at least once; I never follow a recipe; I can explain the difference between poached and boiled."*

Notes:

Getting Connected Activity #7:
One-Legged Interviews

A lighthearted little activity with a twist to it: to keep the dialogue short, the person who is speaking must stand on one leg!

General Instructions: Direct your students to find two other people in the room – strangers or slight acquaintances (not their best buddies). They form standing triads and introduce themselves to each other. They will be answering a question (of course!) related to the topic that you post on a chart or overhead transparency. Each person gets a chance to answer the question but they have to keep their answers short. To make sure they do this, the person speaking stands on one leg. The other two students in the triad are there to listen and help the speaker balance if necessary. They can answer one or more questions like those in *Mingle Mingle*.

Set-Up/Materials: You can pose the questions verbally or with visuals prepared beforehand. The activity works with large or small groups and takes about 5 minutes depending upon how many questions you ask.

Examples: In a train-the-trainer class, the question was: *"What were your best and worst training experiences?"* At a business marketing workshop, the question became: *"What are your two most successful marketing strategies?"* In a college creative writing course, the question was: *"What kind of writing are you most passionate about and what piece of writing are you working on right now?"* In a high school basic math class the questions included: *"How do you feel about math in general and when do you use math skills in your daily life?"*

Notes:

Getting Connected Activity #8:
Birds-of-a-Feather

This is one of my favorites from **Presenting with Pizzazz.** The variations are limited only by your imagination. You can use this activity during any step of the map as an energizer as well as a review of the material learned.

General Instructions: Students stand and find somebody in the room who likes the same junk food they do. This means that they have to move around the room saying out loud the name of the junk food they like. They form standing pairs (triads are okay too, and I always tell them to make sure no one is left out and to pull any wandering waif into their group) with the person/people who like the same junk food. Then they introduce themselves to each other and – guess what? – answer a question you have written on a chart or overhead transparency. The questions can be the same or similar to the ones for the activity *Mingle Mingle.* You give them about 30 - 60 seconds to talk, then announce they must now find a different partner, someone who likes the same genre of movie or book (adventure, romance, fiction, sci fi, biographical, etc.). Again they pair up, introduce themselves, and answer another question. Do this one or two more times so that they have had a chance to meet at least three people and answer at least three questions. Examples of *Birds of a Feather* phrases are:

Find someone who ...

- *has vacationed in the same place you have;*
- *is wearing the same colored shoes you are;*
- *has the same initial for their middle name;*
- *was born in the same season;*
- *drives the same make or color of car;*
- *likes the same sport;*
- *has the same hobby.*

As you can see, the list can be endless!

Set-Up/Materials: Students will need room to move around. You can post the questions visually on a chart or just say them. Depending upon the length of the dialogue time and number of repetitions, the activity will take from 5 - 10 minutes.

Examples: Some of the questions asked at a real estate review class included: *"What are three things you remember from yesterday's class? What is the most important point to keep in mind when you're closing a sale? What is one piece of information that will change the way you work with prospective clients?"* In a middle school language arts class the questions were: *"How was Tom Sawyer like a light bulb? In your opinion, what was the most exciting part of the story so far? What is one conflict that needs to be resolved by the end of the story?"* Remember to vary the questions and always relate them to the topic.

Notes:

Getting Connected #9:
Walking Bingo

This is a variation on the *People Hunt* that is even more content specific and works well as a pre-test/post-test activity.

General Instructions: Each student has a bingo card with items related to the topic written in each square. Students walk around the room and ask each other to give a definition of one of the items on the card. Students can sign the square on another student's card only if they can give a definition for the item in that square. No signature is collected if the person doesn't know what the item is. And no signature is collected unless the person actually explains or defines the item (*"Yes, I know what it means"* doesn't cut it). Each student can sign the same card only once. The goal is to get five signatures in a row. When this happens, the person with the five signatures yells *"Bingo!"* and stands in the front of the room. Let the activity progress until you have a fair number of "bingos". Then give them a round of applause, a little prize related to the topic, or a funny gag gift. You might choose to have the bingo people quickly define the items verbally for the whole group.

Set-Up/Materials: This activity takes a bit of preparation. You need to create "bingo" cards before the class, one per student, with squares in which you've written topics you plan to cover in the class. The only hitch is that you need to vary the places you write in the topics so that the same topic isn't written in the same square for each card. You can also vary the topics so that different ones appear on different cards. I make templates for four different cards, Xerox the cards, and pass them out in random order. Of course you can have your students make their own cards by handing them blank bingo cards. They fill in the squares from a written list of topics you've posted on a chart or overhead transparency. You'll need bingo cards, pens or pencils, and toy gifts. *Walking Bingo* will work with any size group. Modify the rules to accommodate the groups (example: with small groups, people may sign a card twice). Time needed is 5 - 15 minutes depending upon the size of the group, difficulty of the items, and speed of the number of bingos.

Examples: In a college speech class, the cards listed topical items such as: *active participation, signature stories, metaphors, follow-up, platform skills, closings, nonverbal communication, group management.* A middle school Spanish class included Spanish words and phrases on the card. A government welfare reform training had old and new welfare regulations listed in the bingo squares. The bingo card can be used as a pre-test so students can see what they already know and a post-test to see what new things they've learned.

Notes:

Sharing The Wealth Flight Kit

· · · · ·

The goal of these activities is to make your lectures interactive so that your students are involved even as they learn new information. Remember, the activities can be as long or as short as you wish. You can sprinkle your lectures with a quick *Sharing the Wealth* activity every ten to fifteen minutes or so and still have time to cover the material. ***All of these activities connect students to the topic you're presenting through a sharing of information.***

Notes:

Sharing the Wealth Activity #1:
Pair Shares

These little activities are the foundation pieces of any interactive lecture: short, sweet, to-the-point, and incredibly easy to create. In fact, they can be used in all steps of the styles map whenever you want to insert a quick dialogue or review. There are twelve *Pair Shares* in **Presenting with Pizzazz.**

General Instructions: Direct your students to turn to a neighbor (a person sitting next to them, behind them, across from them, to the right or left, etc.) and tell that person one (two, three) things they just learned in the last ten minutes. You make sure no one is left out by letting your students know they can form triads if someone doesn't have a partner. It's as simple as that.

Set-Up/Materials: Nothing special is required. The size of the group doesn't matter. *Pair Share*s can be as short (10 seconds) or as long (1 - 2 minutes) as you wish.

Examples: Other *Pair Shares* from **Presenting with Pizzazz** include: *"Stand up, find a person across the room, introduce yourself, and tell that person the two most important things you learned from the lecture." "Turn to the person behind you and ask that person a question about what has been presented so far. Make sure you know the answer to the question." "If your life depended upon remembering what you just heard, how would you explain it to your executioner? Tell the person sitting in front of you."*

Notes:

Sharing the Wealth Activity #2:
Doodle Drawings

Also referred to by the fancy name of "analog drawing," a doodle represents information in a visual, spatial way. Doodles can also be metaphorical (see the next activity). Doodles are lines, drawings, logos, designs, shapes, anything that stands for a piece of information.

General Instructions: Direct your students to get a piece of scratch paper (or use the margins of their handouts, agendas, books, 3x5 index cards, etc.) and draw a doodle, line, or shape representing one thing they just learned. Give them about 30 - 60 seconds to draw the doodle then show and explain it to a neighbor. If seated in small groups and time permits, students can share their doodles with the small group. Emphasize that this is *NOT* an art contest. It's simply a way of helping them remember the information because pictures are remembered more easily than words.

Set-Up/Materials: Students need scratch paper or 3x5 index cards and pens/pencils to draw with. Colored markers are fun too and add an extra dimension to the drawings. Doodles can also be drawn on sticky post-it notes and stuck to a chart on the wall or to their handouts or books.

Examples: At a customer service training, participants drew doodles that represented three signs of customer satisfaction. In a high school math class, the doodles became a visual way to remember a mathematical formula. In a middle school history class, students drew metaphorical doodles representing characters in *Johnny Tremain.*

Notes:

Sharing the Wealth Activity #3:
Metaphors

Whenever you ask; *"How is this like ....?"* and name something unrelated to it, you're creating a metaphor. Metaphorical thinking is a phenomenally creative and useful way to learn because it helps your participants understand and remember the essence of something by comparing it to something else. In fact, our daily language is riddled with metaphors: *"It's raining cats and dogs; He shot out of there like a bolt of lightning; She's two bricks shy of a full load; They're just letting off steam; Cat got your tongue? He thinks he's the big cheese;"* and so on.

General Instructions: You can use metaphors as part of your lecture: *"Planning a budget is like water-skiing because ...,"* *"Customer service is like building a house because ..."*. Or you can ask your students to finish the metaphor: *"How is photosynthesis like a bridge?"* *"Name three ways the main character is like a tornado."* *"How is resume writing like brewing coffee?"* Or your students can create their own metaphors for the topic: they work together in small groups of four - six so that they can bounce ideas off each other. Each group creates a metaphor then explains the metaphor to the whole class. Or groups can draw visuals of their metaphors on chart papers and then explain them. Explaining the metaphor is an important part of the activity as it's in the explanation that your students will deepen their own understanding of the topic. Another way of using a metaphor is to hold up an object and ask the group to come up with five - ten ways the topic is like the object you're holding – they'll *ALWAYS* be able to do it!

Set-Up/Materials: No special set-up is needed unless you want your students to move into small groups. They'll need drawing materials if you want them to create visual metaphors. One of the best sources for small metaphorical toys is **Kipp Brothers Company** (see the *Resources* section in this book). Group size can be small or large.

Examples: During a college history class, the instructor held up her shoe and said, *"How is American history like this shoe?"* In my learning styles workshops I pass out rainbow colored paper sunglasses (from Kipp Brothers) and say, *"Name ten ways learning styles are like these glasses."* In a class on interviewing skills, the trainer asked the participants to explain how interviewing is like eating a new food. In a high school science class, the teacher asked, *"How was this lab experiment like a football game?"*

Notes:

Sharing the Wealth Activity #4:
Pop-Ups

The point of this activity is to do a quick review in a high-energy way in a short amount of time.

General Instructions: At your signal, students randomly "pop up" out of their seats one-at-a-time, say one thing they learned (or already knew or remembered) about the topic, and just as quickly sit down again. If the group is small, set a time limit so that, if everyone pops up within the time limit, everyone gets a little prize of some kind. If the group is large, let them know that everyone gets a prize if at least ten (or fifteen) people pop up within the time limit. Students pop up one-at-a-time. If two pop up at the same time they can take turns speaking then sit down. The competition of students against the clock (the time limit) makes this activity work.

Set-Up/Materials: No special set-up is needed. The time limit is totally up to you and can be as short as 1 - 2 minutes. Group size doesn't matter. You'll need enough little prizes for everyone – like candy, pencils, toys, ("lolli-POPS!") or whatever you think your students would like.

Examples: In a communication skills training with thirty people, the time limit was 3 minutes, the number of pop ups necessary was fifteen, and participants were to share anything they remembered about the communication skills they learned. In a college health class, the time limit was 2 minutes and everyone in the class of ten had to pop up and share one of their own wellness techniques. In an elementary language arts class, students popped up with different parts of speech. In a high school geography class, students listed as many European countries as they could remember in two minutes.

Notes:

Sharing the Wealth Activity #5:
Signals

Simple, fun, and very effective ways to check for under-standing while at the same time reviewing what has been learned.

General Instructions: You demonstrate the following signals to the group: a clap for *"yes,"* a foot stomp for *"no,"* arms folded for *"not sure."* Then you ask a number of questions related to the information you've just taught. Students answer each question with one of the signals. After four or five questions and signals, you continue with the lecture. You can also throw in silly questions or ones that have nothing to do with the topic to create a little humor. Signals are easy to use in any step of the map, especially when you want to make sure everyone understands the instructions for an activity.

Set-Up/Materials: Nothing special is needed.

Examples: I also use thumbs up *("yes"),* thumbs down *("no"),* and a hand drawing circles in the air that means *"Didn't get it, repeat please."* A PE teacher had his students shout, *"Way cool!"* and *"No way!"* You can always use signals to check for understanding when you've given some complicated instructions *("Will you be working with a partner? Do you have 15 minutes to complete the activity? Can you get help from other groups? Will you be presenting your project to the class?").* You can tell by the signals if you need to repeat any of the instructions.

Notes:

Sharing the Wealth Activity #6:
Fill-in-the-Blanks

One of the best ways to keep your learners involved while you lecture is to have them take notes by filling in the missing parts of a worksheet.

General Instructions: You hand out worksheets with major points from your lecture written on them. Key words have been left out and it's the students' job to fill in the key words as they listen to the lecture. Afterwards, you may want to review the key words with them.

Set-Up/Materials: Worksheets with fill-in-the-blank sections prepared in advance and pens or pencils.

Examples: I've seen trainers do this with a workshop agenda as well as with lecture content. One corporate trainer uses fill-in-the-blanks as review throughout his entire two-day training. Another has participants try to fill-in-the-blanks before the lecture (to assess what they already know), then check or change their answers during the lecture.

Notes:

Sharing the Wealth Activity #7: Personal Reflections

You can find eight of these thoughtful little pauses in **Presenting with Pizzazz.** The point is to create a quiet minute or two for your students to think and write during your lecture.

General Instructions: The simplest *Personal Reflection* is to direct your students to take one minute and write a sentence describing what they've just learned. Or ask them to write three things they remember from the lecture, then circle (or put a star, check mark, or dot beside) the most important one. This way they begin to analyze what they've learned.

Examples: Other variations include writing a question about or reaction to the information learned, summing up the lecture in a written word or phrase, or quietly reviewing written material and highlighting or writing notes about it.

Notes:

Sharing the Wealth Activity #8:
Pop Quiz

A great way to generate interest in an upcoming lecture before you begin.

General Instructions: Hand out a worksheet that has a series of questions on it (or fill-in-the-blank sentences), all pertaining to information soon-to-be-learned. Give students a certain time limit (usually about 3-5 minutes) to answer as many of the questions as they can. Encourage "cheating," i.e. they can look through materials, put their heads together, get answers from other groups, etc. After time is called, they can use the pop quiz as a note-taking page during the lecture. Or they can refer to it and check/correct their answers as you give them the information.

Set-Up/Materials: You'll need to prepare the *Pop Quiz* worksheet in advance. Students will need writing materials.

Examples: David Meier, in his **Accelerated Learning Training Methods Workshop,** uses this technique to enhance a lesson in ordering French food. He passes out a list of twenty French words to translate before the lesson. The *Pop Quiz* becomes a post-test too, as his training participants compare what they knew before the lesson to what they know after it.

Notes:

Making It Happen Flight Kit

• • • • •

These activities help students use and review the information they've learned. If the lesson doesn't lend itself to practical skills to master, then you can create projects or activities in which your students use the information in a variety of ways. A reminder: *Making It Happen* activities can take place outside the classroom too. **The goal of these activities is for students to do something with what they've learned.**

Notes:

Making It Happen Activity #1:
Learning Stations

One of the most fun and fast-moving ways to practice skills when you have a large enough group to work with (15 or more). Besides practicing skills, *Learning Stations* can also be used to review information or present new information – *and all at the same time!*

General Instructions: You create a number of "learning stations" around the room before the activity begins. Stations are tables at which a small group will sit and practice a skill related to the subject just taught. You post the directions for each station on a chart paper or handout located at the station. All materials for each station need to be there also. Divide your students into small groups and assign each group a station at which to begin. They'll practice the skill at their respective station until time is called. Then groups rotate clockwise around the room, going to the next station. Rotations continue at a timed pace until all groups have experienced all stations.

Set-Up/Materials: This activity takes some planning as you'll need to have all station materials and instructions set up beforehand. Station groups can be as small as two or three students or as large as six to eight students. Be sure to have enough materials at each station for all learners. Station time can last from 5 - 20 minutes depending upon the number of stations you have and the skills students are practicing. Use upbeat music to signal rotations. If the entire *Learning Stations* activity lasts longer than 90 minutes, you might want to build in a short bathroom break.

Examples: At one of my communication skills trainings, thirty participants, in small groups of five, rotated around six stations. At each 10 minute station they practiced one communication skill. During a train-the-trainer course, the trainees created a presentation at one station to be shown to the class after the station time was over. At the same training, the instructor used another station to teach body language awareness. A guest trainer was called in to answer questions at a third station, and participants reviewed training skills at the fourth and fifth stations. In other words, the stations included presentation planning, skills practice, a review of old information, learning new information, and a question/ answer session – *and all at the same time.*

Notes:

Making It Happen Activity #2:
Each One, Teach One

A simple but effective skills practice activity based on the **Presenting with Pizzazz** tip: *"You master what you teach."*

General Instructions: For this activity, students need to work in pairs. One person becomes the "teacher" and one the "learner." The teacher instructs the learner in the skill and has him practice it. Then they switch roles and the new teacher instructs the new learner in another skill to practice.

Set-Up/Materials: Nothing special is needed.

Examples: A high school math instructor had her students pair up and teach each other how to solve a calculus equation. An insurance company computer trainer had his training participants walk each other through steps in a new software program, taking turns telling it and doing it on the computer. Students in an elementary class taught each other social etiquette relating to eating in the cafeteria.

Notes:

Making It Happen Activity #3:
Roundtable Review:

An interesting way to check for understanding while reviewing what's been learned.

General Instructions: Students are seated in small groups. Each student writes his name and a sentence describing part of what he's learned on a blank piece of paper. Then all the students in the small group pass their papers clockwise to the persons next to them. They all write another sentence about what they've learned on their neighbors' papers. Again they pass the papers and continue writing and passing until they receive their own paper once more. After each person has gotten his own paper back, he reads it and shares any questions, reactions, or final thoughts with his small group. If you wish, you can have volunteers read one or two of the written statements.

Set-Up/Materials: Each person will need writing materials. Time can be 5 - 15 minutes depending upon the size of the small groups.

Examples: Instead of making it open-ended, you can direct the learners as to what to write each time by posting ideas on a chart or overhead transparency: *"What's the most important thing you learned? What are three skills you can use? What's the least important thing you learned? Describe one of the skills you plan to use. What is one question you still have?"* Or they can write specific steps to a certain skill, or they can write a question for their neighbor to answer. They write the answer, pass the paper, and write another question on the next one. One final variation is doing the activity as a whole class, with students walking around and writing on each other's papers in a random fashion for a specific length of time.

Notes:

Making It Happen Activity #4:
Four-On-The-Floor

A variation of *Gallery Walk* using the floor instead of the walls.

General Instructions: Large chart papers are taped to the floor in the four corners of the room. The charts are labeled with specific topics addressed in the lecture or with four specific skills related to the topics. Divide your students into four smaller groups. Each group begins in a different corner and, staying together, rotates around all four corners. In each corner the group discusses what they know about the topic or skill and writes the two (or three) most important things on the floor chart. As they rotate, the groups must think of things to write that haven't already been written on the charts. When the rotations have been completed, the students walk around one more time reading the floor charts and taking notes about what they observe. They discuss their notes in their small groups. You may want to close with a quick large group discussion.

Set-Up/Materials: You'll need to prepare the floor charts before the activity. Your students will need space to move around the room and note-taking materials, including felt pens with which to write on the charts.

Examples: At a business seminar, floor charts were labeled with four customer service-related skills: *handling complaints, meeting new customers, follow-up, phone etiquette.* At a teacher's workshop, charts were labeled with assessment strategies: *subjective, objective, individual, group.* In a high school literature class, the corners stood for four literary works the class had read.

Notes:

Making It Happen Activity #5:
Game Boards

This one takes some preparation time but pays off with high-interest involvement.

General Instructions: Learners are divided into small groups. Each group receives a "game board" and "game cards." The groups have a set time in which they read, discuss, and sort out the game cards according to the categories in which they go. Students in each group must come to an agreement before each card is placed in a category on the game board. When finished, the groups check their answers and give themselves a group "high five" for effort.

Set-Up/Materials: Students form groups of 3 - 6 depending upon the size of the class. You'll need to create the game boards, cards, and answer keys prior to the class. You'll need enough copies of the boards, cards, and keys so that each group has its own. Time for the activity ranges from 15 - 30 minutes depending upon the complexity of the *Game Board* activity, the number of cards that need sorting, and the discussion time afterwards.

Examples: In a workforce development class, the game board categories were transferable skills *(technology, systems, interpersonal, resources, foundation skills, etc.)* and the game cards described job seekers or job opportunities related to those skills. In an elementary science class, the game board categories were: *mammals, insects, reptiles, and birds.* Of course the cards named various living creatures. In a teacher training, student-teachers created their own game board showing the steps of effective lesson design, and they sorted cards that described each step.

Notes:

Making It Happen Activity #6:
Victorious Vignettes

For students who like role-play or dramatizing life-related situations. Also a great activity for simulated skills practice.

General Instructions: Although *Victorious Vignettes* can be done in pairs, it's probably more effective to divide students into groups of 4 or more (they can bounce ideas off each other and shy learners can take less conspicuous roles). Each group plans a short skit or role-play simulating a real-life situation in which they use the information or a skill they learned in the class. The whole class applauds each presentation. You can lead a short discussion after each skit if appropriate.

Set-Up/Materials: Students need enough space to present their skits and any extra props required. They'll also need about 10 - 15 minutes to create their role-plays and about 2 - 5 minutes per group to present them to the whole class.

Examples: In a middle school history class, the skits all revolved around the issue of slavery with different groups acting out different ideologies. In a community college investment class, the role-plays became sales pitches for different investment plans. In a conflict management training, the presentations showed on-the-job conflicts that were resolved using the skills learned in the training.

Notes:

Making It Happen Activity #7:
Game Show

A high energy way of reviewing information using any number of popular television game show formats. Keep the competition light, have groups compete against groups instead of individuals against individuals, and make sure that everyone gets a chance to play.

General Instructions: Choose a game show format (*Jeopardy, Hollywood Squares, Concentration,* or *The Big Spin* are some good ones) and adapt it to your class, subject matter, timeline, etc. For *Jeopardy,* categories all relate to what's been taught and you ask questions pertaining to each category. Instead of asking individuals to answer the questions, make it a group competition where groups have to put their heads together to come up with an answer they all agree with. And make it a win-win for everyone with some kind of consolation prize for the groups that don't come in first. Again a reminder, keep the competition lighthearted and fun with everyone cheering everyone else. It needs to feel fun and safe for all, otherwise you'll have students quietly withdrawing from the game or taking over to win at all costs.

Set-Up/Materials: You'll need to make the game show materials beforehand with enough questions to fill in the time allotted for the review. Toy prizes (enough for everyone) are fun souvenirs of the game.

Examples: In an elementary math class, the *Concentration* game match-up cards were math facts and student groups took turns choosing which two cards to turn over. In a real estate course, the *Jeopardy* categories related to sections of the real estate textbook, the questions were of varying degrees of difficulty, and students worked in groups of three to answer the questions. In fact, in that class, all groups could get points for the right answers so all groups could be winners.

Notes:

Making It Happen Activity #8:
Bringing It Home

Especially applicable for ongoing classes and trainings, this activity is done outside the learning environment. Teaching someone else a learned skill reinforces the learning for the one who's teaching the skill.

General Instructions: Students decide upon a person to whom they will teach a skill learned in the class. It can be a fellow student, friend, or family member. Students teach the skill to this person outside the learning environment, then they report to the class the results of the instruction. You can direct them to have the person who learns the new skill write a short summary of what they learned and how effective the instruction was. Or students can bring their friend or family member into the classroom to demonstrate what they learned.

Set-Up/Materials: Nothing special is necessary unless you want your students to keep a specific record of the results of the activity.

Examples: In a communication skills training, participants taught co-workers the skill of active listening. In a college speech class, students taught a nonverbal communication game to friends. In a high school biology class, students showed family members how to use a microscope. Another variation of *Bringing It Home* is to have students practice a certain skill for a period of time while keeping a journal or record of the results of each practice session.

Notes:

Making It Happen Activity #9:
Card Swap

A more quiet, reflective way of using information learned in a class or training.

General Instructions: Each student takes a 3 x 5 index card and writes a description of a situation related to what's being learned in the class. The situation can be a problem that needs solving, a question to answer, a specific real-life experience, or a way of using the information learned. Then students pair up and exchange cards. They read their partner's card and write a response on it. They return the card to their partner and read and discuss the responses together. Or you can direct them to exchange cards with a new partner to get another response. You can have them exchange cards a few times until they have four or five responses to read on their own cards (they may have to use a number of 3 x 5 cards).

Set-Up/Materials: No special set-up is necessary. Students need 3 x 5 cards (at least 3 per student) and writing materials.

Examples: In a conflict management training, participants wrote about real-life conflicts they wanted help in solving. They worked in small groups, passing their conflict cards to another group to discuss, solve, and write responses. Then the cards were returned to the original groups to read and discuss the responses. In a high school foreign language class, each student wrote a few questions on his card for another student to answer. In an elementary class reviewing the New England states, each student wrote the name of one state on his card and other students wrote facts they remembered about the state.

Notes:

Celebrating Success
Flight Kit
• • • • •

These activities connect students to future possibilities even while they celebrate what they've learned together. Again, a reminder: many *Celebrating Success* activities can be done outside of the learning environment. *The goal of these activities is to wrap up the learning and bring it home in memorable ways.*

For many of these activities, you'll need an art table filled with 3-dimensional art materials. You can use everyday stuff from home and school (tape, colored paper, string, paper plates, styrofoam cups, straws, etc.) or inexpensive supplies from a craft store: beads, colored feathers, sparkly pipe cleaners, doilies, colored cord, yarn, wooden sticks, stickers, sequin, modeling clay, etc. One of the best sculpting clays is *Model Magic* (see the *Resources* section at the end of this book) – clean, odorless, non-sticky, white (almost the texture of smooth moldable styrofoam), and it can be colored with felt pens while air-drying.

Notes:

Celebrating Success Activity #1:
Koosh Throw

A quick and simple closing activity that actually can be used during any step of the map.

General Instructions: The group stands in a large circle and a koosh ball, nerf ball, or similar soft object is thrown randomly around the circle. As students catch the ball, they share the most important thing they've learned or what they plan to do with what they've learned. A nice touch is for them to acknowledge and compliment individuals or the whole group for the time they spent learning together.

Set-Up/Materials: If the group is really large (30 or more), you can divide them into two standing groups each with its own koosh ball. If there isn't enough space to make a standing circle, students can stand by their chairs. You'll need something soft to throw (besides koosh and nerf balls, nylon bath loofah balls work really well as do small stuffed animals).

Examples: At a customer service training, participants shared the customer service skill they planned to practice the next day. In a college job skills class, students thanked each other for specific help they received during the session. In a middle school science class, students shared the hypotheses they planned to test as part of a homework project.

Notes:

Celebrating Success Activity #2:
Sculpt It

A wonderfully creative way to make a three-dimensional reminder of the learning.

General Instructions: Using *Play Dough, Model Magic,* modeling clay, or any three-dimensional art material, each student sculpts a representation of what he has learned in the class or training. The sculpture can be metaphorical as well as representational. Participants take turns showing and explaining their sculptures to the large group or within small groups.

Set-Up/Materials: Students need 3-dimensional art materials and enough time allowed to sculpt and share (about 5 - 10 minutes to create, 1 minute per person to share).

Examples: In a closing session for a national teacher's conference, educators used Model Magic and colored felt pens to create starfish to remind them of the moral to Jack Canfield's story about starfish in his book **Chicken Soup for the Soul.** (Don't remember the moral? "It *makes a difference to THIS one.")* During a religious retreat, participants created clay sculptures representing their obstacles to living their faith. In a teacher's class on the topic of the learning cycle, student-teachers made play dough models of cyclical things in their own lives.

Notes:

Celebrating Success Activity #3:
Snowball Fight

This activity bears repeating from **Presenting with Pizzazz** because it's one of the greatest and most high-energy celebration activities around.

General Instructions: Each student takes a blank white piece of typing paper and writes his action plan on it large enough for others to read. Students then form a standing circle. At your direction, they crumple up their papers and begin throwing "snowballs" at each other. They pick up and throw as many snowballs as they can in 30 seconds. When time is called, each person picks up a snowball, opens it, and takes a turn reading the action plan to the whole group.

Set-Up/Materials: You'll need enough blank paper and writing materials for everyone and a large break-out area free of furniture (move the class furniture if you have to). If the group is really big, they can form two standing circles when they read the action plans. Time needed can be from 5 - 20 minutes depending upon the size of the group.

Examples: None needed! Try it and see for yourself!

Notes:

Celebrating Success Activity #4:
Let's Trade!

A neat networking activity, and one that insures follow-up afterwards.

General Instructions: Each student writes his name and phone number on the front of a 3x5 index card (in an adult training, participants can use their own business cards instead). On the back of the card, each student writes his action plan in one or two sentences. Students then form standing pairs and read their action plans to their partners. They exchange cards. They find a new partner to form another standing pair and read the action plan of the card they're holding (not their own this time). Once again, they exchange cards and find a third and final partner. They read the action plans again, exchange cards, and return to their seats with someone else's card. You direct them to give this person a call in one (or two) weeks to see how that person is doing with his action plan.

Set-Up/Materials: No special set-up is needed. Students need 3x5 index cards and pens or pencils. Groups can be large or small. Time is about 5 minutes.

Examples: With students in regular ongoing classes, a homework assignment or community service project could replace the action plan. Or the next day's class could begin with students finding the person whose card they have, and asking that person a question related to what he wrote on his card.

Notes:

Celebrating Success Activity #5:
Inside-Outside Circles

This one needs a large group (thirty or more) to really make it work.

General Instructions: The large group forms two circles, one inside the other, with the same number of people in each circle (you may have to participate if there is an odd number of students). The inside circle turns around to face the outside circle so that standing pairs are formed. You direct them to tell their partner the most important thing they learned from the class or lesson. Then they shake hands, say goodby, and rotate as you say, *"Inside circle, move right three people."* They form a new standing pair and share what they plan to do with what they've learned. You give another rotation direction *("Outside circle, move right five people.")* Again, they shake hands, say goodby, and rotate. You can repeat this procedure as many times as you wish, with different statements or questions to dialogue about and different rotation directions.

Set-Up/Materials: No materials are needed but a large break-out area free of furniture is necessary. The activity can take anywhere from 10 - 20 minutes to do.

Examples: I've asked students to come up with things to share as well as rotation directions. They've included: *complementing each other, next steps in learning more about the subject, questions they still have, how they feel about what they learned, who they plan to share the information with, the best part and the worst part of the learning experience, who they really got to know and how they plan to stay in touch.* Some of their rotation directions got a little crazy: *"Inside and outside circles rotate right six people at the same time; Inside circle right one person and outside circle left one person (they'll rotate in the same direction!)."*

Notes:

Celebrating Success Activity #6:
Human Machines

A wildly moving celebration that gets hoots and hollers from participants and onlookers alike.

General Instructions: Learners form groups of 5 - 7 people. Each group is given about ten minutes to plan the creation of a human machine (using their bodies, movements, and sounds) that represents something to do with the information learned. The machine can be real or imaginary. Each person in the small group must be a part of the machine and represent his part with a sound and a movement. When the groups are ready, they take turns acting out their machine. Onlookers can guess what they are or the small group can explain their machine to the whole group while they're doing it. End each human machine presentation with a rousing round of applause.

Set-Up/Materials: No special materials are required unless you want to furnish some extra props such as hats, balloons, noisemakers, etc. A break-out area free of furniture will be needed for the presentations.

Examples: Some of the human machines I've seen included metaphors for the learning such as trains, computers, jack-in-the-boxes, merry-go-rounds, and typewriters. Other representational and imaginary machines included a communicating machine, a fortune-telling machine, an excuse-making machine, a math homework machine, a customer service machine, a stress-breaker machine, a surfing-the-net machine, and a time management machine.

Notes:

Celebrating Success Activity #7:
Pats-on-the-Back

A warm way of giving and getting celebration compliments while standing up and moving around.

General Instructions: Each student traces his own hand (an enlarged version) with bright felt pen on a blank piece of standard-sized colored construction paper. He prints his name in large letters in the middle of the hand. Then he tapes or pins (with help if necessary) the construction paper hand to his back. While upbeat music plays, students walk around the room giving each other "pats-on-the-back" by writing compliments on each others papers. Human chains will begin to form as one student writes on one back while someone else is writing on his! When you call time, they take their pats-on-the-back home with them as souvenirs.

Set-Up/Materials: Construction paper, felt pens, writing pens or pencils, music, and room to move around in are all needed to make this activity work. It can take anywhere from 10 - 30 minutes depending upon the size of the group and how into it they are.

Notes:

Celebrating Success Activity #8:
Bag It!

A variation of *Pats-On-The-Back* using paper lunch bags instead of construction paper.

General Instructions: Each student decorates a blank white standard-sized paper lunch bag with his name in bright colors (3-dimensional art materials are optional). As upbeat music plays, students move around the room exchanging bags and writing compliments on each other's bags. They can also write their action plans on their own bags. After the activity is over, students put their materials and any other little souvenir items (toys, candy, certificates, prizes, etc.) in their bags to take home.

Set-Up/Materials: You can buy blank white lunch bags in bulk at most wholesale stores such as Costco or Price Club. You'll also need felt pens and markers, pens or pencils, music, and little prizes, toys, or certificates to put into the bags. 3-dimensional art materials add a fun touch to the bag decorating.

Examples: For long-term classes, I've had my students make little things for each other (inspirational sayings on slips of paper, trinkets from natural materials, whatever they like to make) and bring them to the last class to put into the bags – gifting each other with something special that represents them. The "gifting ceremony" was held at the end of the last class with students sitting in a circle and taking turns telling about their gifts before passing them out to the others.

Notes:

Celebrating Success Activity #9:
Vision Sticks

A serious and thoughtful ceremony based on a Native American ritual. You might explain before the activity that this was a way ancient Native Americans set goals for themselves.

General Instructions: Each student has a dowel stick about 6 inches in length, a skinny strip of blank paper about the same length, and 3-D art materials of his choosing. He writes his goal for himself (it can be his specific action plan or a more general life goal) on the strip of paper and winds it around the stick. Then he decorates the stick with art materials that are pleasing to him so that the paper can't be seen and the stick is covered. Soft background music sets the quiet reflective mood. When all students are finished decorating their vision sticks, they sit together in a circle and take turns sharing their vision sticks and goals if they wish. A lovely word to end the little ceremony with is to have everyone stand and say in unison; *"Namaste,"* which, roughly translated from a Native American language, means: *"The spirit in me honors and greets the spirit in you."*

Set-Up/Materials: Besides craft store art materials, students can also use natural items such as leaves, raffia, leather strips, bark, bird feathers, twigs, small rocks, etc. Dowel sticks (from a craft store, 5/16 inch diameter and cut into 6 inch lengths) or short plant branches, strips of paper, writing materials, tape, glue, and music, are all necessary items. Allow enough time to create the vision sticks (at least 10 - 15 minutes) as well as to share them in the group (about one minute per person). This activity works best when learners have been with each other for awhile in an ongoing class or training.

Notes:

Celebrating Success Activity #10:
A Letter to Yourself

Many trainers use this activity as part of their training participants' commitment to an action plan.

General Instructions: Each student writes a letter to herself stating what she plans to do with what she's learned and what she thinks the outcomes will be. She can also write a compliment to herself in the letter. Then she signs it, puts it in an envelope, seals it, and addresses it to herself. You collect all the envelopes and mail them in about two to three weeks.

Set-Up/Materials: Letter-writing materials are needed. If you want to get fancy, students can decorate their letters with stickers, markers, glitter, stamps, etc. Time limit will depend on the length of the letters: 5 minutes for a postcard, 10 minutes for a regular letter, 30 minutes or more if you have participants exchange letters and write words of encouragement on each other's letters. Cost of postage can be an obstacle and should be arranged before you do this one (you can cover it or you can ask each learner to bring in a stamp).

Examples: You can write a word of encouragement on the back of the envelopes before you mail them – a nice personal touch! Or you can have the learners leave the envelopes unsealed and you put a small inspirational quote or toy in each one before mailing.

Notes:

Celebrating Success Activity #11:
Four Square Feedback

A great way to get honest feedback from your students while having them think about what they've learned.

General Instructions: Each student takes a blank piece of standard sized paper and divides it into four large squares. Each square actually represents one of the four learning styles. The students fill in the following sentences, one per square:

#1 *My feelings about what I learned are ....*

#2 *The most important information was ...*

#3 *I plan to...*

#4 *Another idea, or suggestion I have is ...*

They can sign them or not, as you wish. When finished, they can share their *"I plan to..."* piece if time permits. You then collect all the feedback pages to look over after they leave.

Set-Up/Materials: Writing materials are necessary. Quiet music is nice too.

Examples: If part of an ongoing class or training, you can begin the next session by reading some of the questions, comments, and ideas from the feedback pages. This is a great way to let your students know how much you value their insights.

Notes:

Resources

Want to learn more?

Take the next step:
attend the
Accelerated Learning
Training Methods Workshop!

In Sharon's opinion, the best train-the-trainer workshop anywhere! For corporate, government, and educational organizations, **The Center for Accelerated Learning** offers both in-house and public training programs in accelerated learning techniques. Teachers and trainers can get better results in less time while having more fun than ever in the classroom and training room! **The Accelerated Learning Training Methods Workshop** is one-of-a-kind: a complete teaching and learning system designed to make all learning experiences successful for all learners.

Other products and services offered by **The Center for Accelerated Learning:**

Accelerated Learning Application News: An outstanding newsletter packed with practical tips, ideas, resources, and proven successful accelerated learning techniques from workshop graduates, teachers, and trainers around the world. Sample articles at the website.

Accelerated Learning Course Builder: An exceptionally useful step-by-step kit to help you develop powerful training programs quickly and with great results! Includes over 400 activities that you can easily customize to fit your particular content. Software included helps you build and evaluate complete courses using accelerated learning techniques.

Accelerated Learning Quiz Show: Easy to use software to quickly create learning games with your own subject matter. Free demonstration available at web site.

The Center for Accelerated Learning
David Meier, Director
1103 Wisconsin St., Lake Geneva, WI 53147
Phone: 414-248-7070   Fax: 414-248-1912
E-Mail: alcenter@execpc.com
Web Site: www.execpc.com/~alcenter

Another fine resource for teachers:

The 4MAT© System
created by Excel, Inc.

One of the most innovative lesson design models in education today, **The 4MAT System** offers teachers at all levels a way of organizing instruction that is brain-compatible and learner-centered. **Excel, Inc.** brings this marvelous tool to educators around the world through the following courses and educational materials:

4MAT Level One Training: Learn how to design instruction that meets the needs of all four learning preferences. Explore learning styles, brain dominance, learning diversity, and 4MAT.

4MAT Level Two Training: Expand and deepen your understanding of 4MAT to create concept-based lessons and units.

4MAT Advanced Training: Become a certified 4MAT© trainer for your own in-house staff development programs.

Other training programs include: **The 4MAT Assessment Training, Administrator's Training, Curriculum and Instruction Course, Parent Seminar, and 4MAT Leadership and Management Trainings.**

Educational books, software, and materials include: **About Learning** by Bernice McCarthy (the definitive book on teaching to learning diversity), **4MATION©** (highly practical and useful 4MAT lesson design software), the **Learning Type Measure©** (an informative learning styles inventory), and more. (**4MAT, 4MATION,** and the **Learning Type Measure** are registered trademarks of Excel, Inc.)

Excel, Inc.
Bernice McCarthy, President
23385 Old Barrington Road, Barrington, IL 60010
Phone: 800-822-4628   Fax: 847-382-4510
E-Mail: michael@excelcorp.com
Web Site: www.excelcorp.com

A valuable resource for trainers:

Creative Training Techniques International, Inc.

Creative Training Techniques International, Inc. specializes in developing innovative train-the-trainer seminars and publications. Their focus is to help clients achieve exceptional results using an eye-opening, revolutionary alternative to lecture-based learning called **Participant-Centered Training.**

Creative Training Techniques International, Inc. seminars and publications include:

Public Seminars: 65,000 trainers have attended Bob Pike's **Creative Training Techniques Public Seminar.** Over 140 seminars are offered in 40 U.S. cities each year.

In-House Training Seminars: Customized programs for trainers, staff, and technical presenters developed for hundreds of organizations.

Annual Train-the-Trainer Conference: Focuses on the power of participant-centered techniques to dramatically increase retention and training transfer to the job.

Creative Solutions Catalog: Filled with fun, stimulating, creative resources including games, magic, music, wuzzles, books, tapes, videos, software, and presentation graphics.

Creative Training Techniques International, Inc.
Robert W. Pike, CSP, President
7620 West 78th Street
Minneapolis, MN 55439
Phone: 800-383-9210 or 612-829-1954
Fax. 612-829-0260
Web Site: www.cttbobpike.com
E-Mail: marketing@cttbobpike.com

And of course,
the author as a resource!

Sharon wants you to know:

- she offers trainings in brain-based learning and teaching, communication, stress management, change, teambuilding, and more *(call her at 775-749-5247 for training information)*;
- she relishes being the "guide-on-the-side," not the "sage-on-the-stage";
- all the effective teaching strategies she used successfully in twenty-three years of classroom instruction (grades kindergarten through high school with Special Education, Gifted and Talented, and English as a Second Language thrown in for good measure) work equally well with adults;
- she "walks her talk" so her classes and trainings are all learner-centered – she models everything she writes about;
- she's taught adults in community college classes, university extension courses, work force development and employment and training programs, community programs, and corporate trainings for almost as long as she's taught kids;
- you can reach her at:

Sharon Bowman, M.A.
P.O Box 464
Glenbrook NV 89413
Phone and Fax: 775-749-5247
E-Mail: SBowperson@aol.com

- she feels thrilled about learning to fly and writing two books;
- finally, when the teacher is ready, the students will come (adapted from *A Course in Miracles*).

Other great resources:

Suppliers of training products and services as well as excellent in-house training programs and public seminars. Call for catalogues and brochures.

The Brain Store
Eric and Diane Jensen, Owners
11080 Roselle St., Suite F
San Diego, CA 92121
Phone: 800-325-4769 • Fax: 619-546-7560

Creative Training Techniques Newsletter
Lakewood Publications
50 S. 9th Street, Minneapolis, MN 55402
Phone: 800-328-4329 • Fax: 612-340-4819

FYI: For Your Inspiration (newsletter)
Training Systems, Inc.
Carolyn B. Thompson, President
221 Vermont Road
Frankfort, IL 60423
Phone: 815-469-1162 • Fax: 815-469-0886

The Humor & Happiness Catalog
Published by: Edward Leigh Enterprises, Inc.
Edward Leigh, M.A., President
P.O. Box 18819
Cleveland, OH 44118
Phone: 800-677-3256 • Fax: 216-291-9450

Kipp Catalog
Kipp Brothers, Inc.
240-242 So. Meridian St.
P.O. Box 157
Indianapolis, IN 46206
Phone: 800-428-1153 • Fax: 800-832-5477

Lakeshore Learning Materials
(suppliers of *Model Magic*)
2695 East Dominguez St.
P.O. Box 6261
Carson, CA 90749
Phone: 800-421-5354 • Fax: 301-537-5403

The Coughlin Company
Dan Coughlin, President
P.O. Box 21814
St. Louis, MO 63109
Phone: 314-453-8453 • Fax: 314-638-3485

CURTIS Services
Curt L. Hansen: Creativity Unlimited
5160 West Jackson Road
Elwell, MI 48832
Phone: 517-887-8410

The Duvall Center
Joyce Duvall, President
2728 Maynard Drive
Indianapolis, IN 46227
Phone: 317-784-6500 • Fax: 317-787-1750

Joanna Slan, Professional Speaker and Trainer
7 Ailanthus Court
Chesterfield, MO 63005
Phone: 800-356-2220 • Fax: 314-530-7970

OMTI Professional Development Services
Ralph Kraus, Director of Programs
2700 E. Dublin-Granville Rd., Suite 7
Columbus, OH 43231
Phone: 800-232-2579 • Fax: 614-895-7401

Partners in Success
Personal and Professional Development
Edwina Frazier, Owner
2644 Lovington Ave.
Troy, MI 48083
Phone: 248-583-3068

The Starting Point
Professional Training for Entrepreneurs
Adele J. Foster, Owner
P.O. Box 124
East Orange, NJ 07019
Phone: 973-763-6782

Order Form

(Need some more books for your friends, co-workers, school, business?)

How To Give It So They Get It!
copies: _____ $17.95 ea. plus shipping

Presenting with Pizzazz!
copies: _____ $14.95 ea. plus shipping

Shake, Rattle And Roll!
copies: _____ $17.95 ea. plus shipping

For quantity discounts call: 775-749-5247.

Note: shipping cost is $4.00 for the first book and $1.00 for each additional book. Distributor discounts available. Send order form with check or money order payable to:

Sharon Bowman
P.O. Box 464
Glenbrook, NV 89413

Name: _____

Address: _____

City, State, Zip: _____

Phone: _____

Fax/E-Mail: _____

Book Total: _____ Shipping Total: _____

Amount Enclosed: _____

_____ I would like to know more about Sharon's seminars, workshops, and trainings.

For more information about products and services, you can also call or fax Sharon at: 775-749-5247. E-Mail: SBowperson@aol.com

Bibliography

• • • • •

Research drawn on for this book:

Barrett, Susan.
It's All in Your Head.
Free Spirit Publishing Co.,
MN 1985

Bowman, Sharon.
Presenting with Pizzazz.
Bowperson Publishing, NV
1997 (702-749-5247)

Caine, Renate.
***Making Connections:
Teaching and the Human
Brain.*** ASCD,VA 1991

Christopher, Elizabeth.
***Leadership Training
Through Gaming.*** Nichols
Publishing, NY 1987

Community College of Aurora.
One Approach – With Style.
CCA, CO, 1997 (303-360-4830)

Gibbs, Jeanne.
***Tribes: A New Way of
Learning and Being
Together.*** Center Source
Systems, CA 1995
(707-577-8233)

Glasser, William.
The Quality School Teacher.
HarperCollins, NY 1993

Goleman, Daniel. ***Emotional
Intelligence.*** Bantam Books,
NY 1995

Gordon, Lawrence.
***People Types and Tiger
Stripes: A Practical Guide
to Learning Styles.*** Center
for Applications of
Psychological Types,
FL 1982

Hannaford, Carla.
***Smart Moves: Why
Learning is not All in Your
Head.*** Great Ocean
Publishers, VA 1995

Hart, Leslie.
***Human Brain and Human
Learning.*** Books for
Educators, AR 1983

Jensen, Eric.
The Learning Brain.
Turning Point Publishing, CA
1994 (619-755-6670)

Johnson, David and Roger.
***Learning Together and
Alone.*** Prentice-Hall, NJ 1975

Johnson, Spencer.
The One Minute Teacher.
Morrow and Co., NY 1986

Kagan, Spencer.
Cooperative Learning.
Kagan Cooperative Learning,
CA 1994 (800-WEE-CO-OP)

Kiersey, D. and Bates, M.
Please Understand Me.
Prometheus Nemesis, CA 1984

Kolb, David.
Experiential Learning.
Prentice-Hall, Inc. NJ 1984

McCarthy, Bernice.
About Learning.
Excel, Inc., IL 1996
(800-822-4628)

McCarthy, Bernice.
***The 4MAT System:
Teaching to Learning
Styles with Right/Left
Mode Techniques.*** Excel,
Inc., IL 1980 (800-822-4628)

Merrill, David.
***Personal Styles and
Effective Performance.***
Chilton Book Co., PN 1981

Palmer, Parker.
The Company of Strangers.
The Crossroad Publishing
Company, NY 1997

Pike, Robert W., CSP.
***Creative Training
Techniques Handbook,
Second Edition.*** Lakewood
Books, MN 1994

Samples, Bob.
Open Mind, Whole Mind.
Jalmar Press, CA 1987

Tannen, Deborah, Ph.D.
***That's Not What I Meant!
How Conversation Style
Makes or Breaks
Relationships.*** Ballantine
Books, NY 1986

Trent, John and Cindy and
Smalley, Gary and Norma.
The Treasure Tree. Word
Publishing, TX 1992

Williams, Linda.
***Teaching for the Two-
Sided Mind.*** Simon and
Schuster, Inc., NY 1983

Books for trainers:

Bellman, Geoffrey.
***The Consultant's Calling:
Bringing Who You Are to
What You Do.*** Jossey-Bass
Publishers, CA 1990

Gelb, Michael.
Present Yourself. Jalmar
Press, CA 1988

Hoff, Ron.
I Can See You Naked.
Universal Press Syndicate,
KS 1992

Hoff, Ron.
Say It in Six. Andrews and
McMeel, KS 1996

Kushner, Malcolm.
***Successful Presentations
for Dummies.*** IDG Books,
CA 1996

Rozakis, Laurie, Ph.D. ***The
Complete Idiot's Guide to
Speaking in Public with
Confidence.*** Alpha Books,
NY 1995

Saltzman, Joel.
***If You Can Talk, You Can
Write.*** Warner Books, Inc.
NY 1993

Slan, Joanna.
Using Stories and Humor: Grab Your Audience. Allyn & Bacon, MA 1998

Walters, Dottie.
Speak and Grow Rich. Prentice Hall, NJ 1997

Walters, Lilly.
What To Say When You're Dying on the Platform. McGraw-Hill, NY 1995

Winget, Larry.
How to Write a Book One Page at a Time. Win Publications, OK 1996

And some of Sharon's favorites:

Bach, Richard.
Illusions: The Adventures of a Reluctant Messiah. Dell Publishing Co., 1977

Bach, Richard.
Running from Safety. Delta, NY 1994

Bissonnette, Denise.
Beyond Traditional Job Development. Milt Wright & Assc., CA 1994 (800-626-3939)

Bolman, Lee and Deal, Terrence. **Leading with Soul.** Jossey-Bass, CA 1995

Bracey, Hyler.
Managing from the Heart. Delacorte Press, NY 1990

Cameron, Julia.
The Artist's Way: A Spiritual Path to Higher Creativity. G.P. Putnam's Sons, NY 1992

Johnson, Spencer.
One Minute for Myself. Avon Books, NY 1985

Manigault, Sandra.
The Book for Math Empowerment. Godosan Publications, VA 1997 (540-720-0861)

McGee-Cooper, Ann.
Time Management for Unmanageable People. Bantam Books, NY 1994

Peters, Tom.
The Tom Peters Seminar: Crazy Times Call for Crazy Organizations. Vintage Books, NY 1994

Roger, John and McWilliams, Peter. **Do It! Let's Get Off Our Buts.** Prelude Press, CA 1991

Slan, Joanna.
I'm Too Blessed to be Depressed. Slan, MO 1998 (888-BLESSED)

Walsch, Neale.
Conversations with God: An Uncommon Dialogue. G.P. Putnam's Sons, NY 1995

Whyte, David. **The Heart Aroused: Poetry and the Preservation of the Soul in Corporate America.** Doubleday, NY 1994